MW00609473

CASCADE COMPANION

CASCADE COMPANION

By Susan Schwartz
Photography by Bob & Ira Spring

Published by
PACIFIC
Search
BOOKS
715 Harrison Street
Seattle, Washington 98109

Cover and Book Design by Lou Rivera

Cover Photo: Fall color at Picture Lake and Mount Shuksan
in North Cascades National Park.

All rights reserved. No part of this book may be reproduced in any
form without the permission of the publisher.

Copyright © 1976 by Pacific Search Books
International Standard Book Number 0-914718-16-9
Library of Congress Catalog Card Number 76-40369
Manufactured in the United States of America

Acknowledgments

I would like to thank all of the people more expert than I who read parts of this book and offered corrections and suggestions. And I would like to thank my friends who helped and put up with me while I was writing.

Particular thanks are due William N. Bischoff, S.J., research professor of history, Seattle University; Dr. W. Thomas Edmondson, professor of zoology, University of Washington; Susan E. Hansen; Dr. Janet Hohn, botanist; Harry Majors, Jr., historian; Dr. V. Standish Mallory, professor of geology, University of Washington; Lynn Paulson, research technologist, department of zoology, University of Washington; Dr. Charles F. Raymond, assistant professor of geophysics, University of Washington; Frank W. Reanier, retired meteorologist, National Weather Service; and Karyl Winn, curator of manuscripts, University of Washington manuscript library.

A still greater debt is owed to the many authors who did the detailed research that made a general book like this one possible.

The responsibility for mistakes, of course, is my own.

S.S.

The Cascades Today

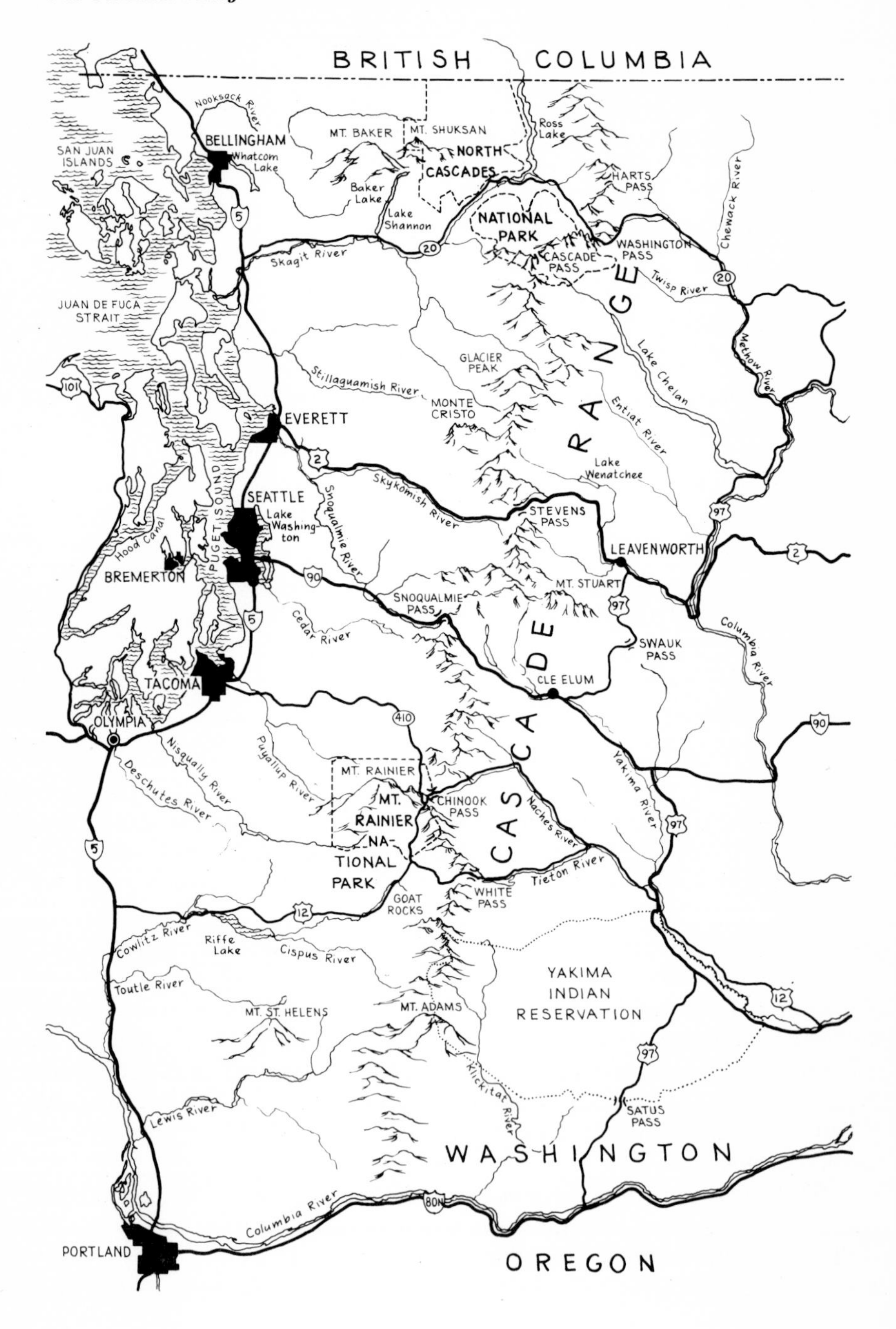

Table of Contents

At 10,000 feet, a view of Mount Adams and the Tatoosh Range from Mount Rainier.

Introduction

Snow Creek in the Enchantment Lakes area.

The Cascade Mountains, one of the rugged, young ranges of the North American West, run from the low Coast Range in southern British Columbia southward through Washington and Oregon to join the Sierra Nevada in northern California.

The highest and most spectacular parts of this range lie within the state of Washington. Here, the mountains run north to south through the state like a ruined wall, dropping from glacier-capped pinnacles averaging 8,000 feet high in the north to gentler, rounded mountains averaging 3,500 feet in the south. Towering above the main range are five volcanoes, including Mount Rainier, the highest volcano in the United States outside Alaska.

There is more than beauty alone to enjoy in the spectacular and varied Cascade range. This mountain wall profoundly affects both natural and human history. The aim of this book is to acquaint you with the wealth of Cascade natural life and history as you wander through the range.

You can find lakes and rocks hung with Indian legends, and read the Cascades' true geologic history in rocks and ice. You can see how the mountain barrier almost makes its own weather patterns, and learn to recognize the specialized features that help plants and animals survive in different parts of the range. And you can learn the tales behind hiking trails and abandoned mines, behind highways and dams and the scars left by logging.

Understanding more of what you see will make the Cascades more beautiful, whether you climb or backpack, ski or hunt, park in a campground, travel the foothills by foot or snowmobile, or simply drive across the passes.

This book is only a beginning. There is much it does not tell — and there is still more we do not even know about the Washington Cascades.

The Weathermakers

Mount Rainier's Ricksecker Point and the upper Nisqually River after a March storm.

The Cascades help to make their own weather. You can see them at it when peaks are cloud-wrapped and lowland towns are clear, when the tops of sleeping volcanoes float like islands above a sea of morning clouds. You can observe the results in the lush forests of the western slopes and the sparse woods of the east. The mountains' complex relationships with the weather produce radically different climates and environments for plant and animal life.

Icy, Windy Peaks

The most obvious climatic difference you will see — even in looking from a city window toward the Cascades — is the temperature difference between mountaintops and lowlands. The highest peaks are crowned with unmelting glaciers and snowfields. The thin upper atmosphere, with only scattered mountaintops to help absorb and hold heat, is colder than the denser, dustier, insulating, and heat-absorbing lower air, where warmth is absorbed by the ground and returned to the atmosphere.

The Cascade peaks are also windier than the lowlands. Because upper air is not slowed by friction or eddies from the ground, it usually travels faster than air at lower elevations. Standing on high lookouts, you can feel this wind and see it in bent and twisted trees. In addition, winds whistle through mountain peaks especially fast because the funneled air speeds up just like a river rushing through a narrow canyon.

Wet West, Dry East

Another obvious difference in Cascade climates relates to moisture: the west side is much wetter than the east. On both sides, however, the peaks are wetter than the lowlands, with the greatest amount of rain and snow a bit west of the Cascade crest.

In Washington, prevailing southwest winds roll warm, moist air inland from the Pacific Ocean. As this air is forced up across the Cascades, it cools. Because cool air cannot hold as much moisture as warm air, clouds, fog, rain, and snow form on the west slopes of the Cascades. The results are lush forests and closely set streams.

At the summit of the range the process is reversed: the air flowing down the eastern slopes is compressed by the growing weight of the atmosphere above it. It takes on heat. The clouds dissipate; the remaining moisture seldom condenses as rain or snow. The result is the dry, sunny climate of the eastern Cascades, with few streams, sparse forest, light snowpack, stretches of grasslands, and even sagebrush desert.

Chinooks and Thunderbolts

One extreme result of the rise and fall of air crossing the mountains is the sometimes friendly, sometimes fearsome chinook wind. The chinook starts as a warm, wet winter or spring wind from the Pacific. Loss of water, as snow or rain, slows its rate of cooling as the air rises, the condensation releasing heat into the surrounding atmosphere. Thus, the chinook sometimes reaches Cascade peaks while still relatively warm — but with its moisture depleted. When this air sweeps down the eastern side of the range, growing still warmer as it is pressed under more and more air above it, it can become a hot, dry torrent melting and evaporating winter snow within hours. The warm chinooks can green a mountain, save starving animals, or set off deadly avalanches.

Another extreme result of air's rise and fall near the peaks is mountain thunder and lightning storms, much more common in the Cascades than in nearby lowlands. In very simple terms, fast-rising air generates chill, unstable air masses that become thunderclouds, and the peaks, like gigantic lightning rods, attract lightning by their very nearness to the clouds. Like the chinooks, summer lightning storms in the Cascades have effects we can see: they have started forest fires that can burn thousands of acres.

Lightning strikes a mountain peak.

Sunrise from Glacier Peak. Fog layers cover the Suiattle River Valley.

Mountain Breezes

A regular pattern of gentler winds is more likely to be familiar to the Cascades traveler than are chinooks or thunderstorms. In the mountains, breezes often begin to blow uphill shortly after sunrise and continue to waft upslope all day. Sometimes flat fog layers fill the valleys in early morning; these clouds usually "burn off" as the sun warms the air enough to evaporate the water droplets, or when air currents carry the moisture away. As the day lengthens, fluffy clouds may hide the tops of the peaks, while the rest of the sky remains clear. At sunset these clouds may drop away, unveiling icefalls and snowfields stained rose by the evening sun. This pattern is not much different from the rise of warm air and the fall of cold air in a house heated by a furnace. The sun acts like a furnace, heating the high peaks through air that is thin and clear. Even when the sun is low, as it is much of the year in northern regions like Washington, its rays hit a steep south-facing mountain slope almost at right angles. As a result, the Cascade peaks heat up more quickly than shady valleys with their thicker, dustier air.

At dusk, you will often notice that breezes begin flowing downhill. Heat escapes through the thin, clean air of the peaks faster than it leaves the heavier, dustier atmosphere of valleys. Cold air at the peaks begins to fall, resulting in nighttime downhill breezes. In a valley with a narrow mouth, a lipped basin, or even a small hollow a few feet across, the heavy cold air may form a "lake" of air several degrees colder than a nearby slope. Lingering snow and late-blooming flowers may be signs of such "cold-air traps." The hollows are likely to make shivery campsites, too.

Smaller Climates

In the thin, high-altitude air of the Cascades, you are likely to get a quick sunburn owing to the relatively unfiltered and intense rays of the sun. This thin air also explains why mountaintops are often so hot in the daytime and so cold at night, and why high-mountain shade is so cold, even on a sunny day. Though mountain rocks may heat quickly in the intense sun, the thin air cannot hold the heat of the sun's rays. The result is a climate of extremes.

There are many other small variations in climates in the Cascades. Slopes facing different directions provide good examples. The exposure may produce trees on one side of a hill and grass on the other. There may be moss growing on only one side of a rock, or panes of ice on one side and alpine flowers on the other. The Cascades are in the Northern Hemisphere and thus receive sunshine mostly from the south. As a result, south-facing slopes of these mountains are warmer and drier than those facing north. West-facing slopes receive more warming and drying, in comparison with those facing east, because the afternoon sun hits a surface that is, in effect, preheated. These differences affect plant life throughout the Cascades.

Just as a climate affects what grows, what grows affects climate — although to a lesser degree. Forests, for example, slow the wind and shade the ground. The dark-colored trees absorb heat during the day and release it slowly at night. The result is a less extreme climate than that of a nearby clearing: a little less windy, a little cooler in daytime, a few degrees warmer at night. Clearings, with no trees to slow heat loss from the ground, receive more dew and frost at night than do forests — a fact that can affect campers as well as plants. Climates that plants can wrap about themselves, even the tiny climate created by hairs on a plant leaf, can be vital to a plant's survival in the extreme heat, cold, and storms of the mountain world.

Jagged Mount Degenhardt in the Southern Picket Range of North Cascades National Park.

The Shaping of the Mountains

Once there was no Cascade Range, according to an Indian tale. The earth stretched flat and dry from the shore of the Pacific. The people were hungry on this barren land. They asked Ocean to help them, so Ocean sent his children, Clouds and Rain, to make streams flow and roots and berries grow.

But the people living in what is now the land east of the Cascades were greedy. They would not let Clouds and Rain go home. They dug deep pits — one of them is fifty-five-mile-long Lake Chelan — and told Clouds and Rain to fill them.

Ocean then grew angry. He scooped up earth to make a wall between himself and those people. The wall is the Cascade Range, and the hole is Puget Sound, the long, narrow inland sea west of the mountains. Although Clouds and Rain still often visit west of the Cascades, where the climate is mild and damp, they seldom go to the near-desert east of the mountains.

There is some truth to this tale. For most of the earth's history, the Cascades and Puget Sound did not exist. If the earth's lifetime so far were a twenty-four-hour day ending at midnight, the Cascades that seem so timeless would have risen just two minutes before midnight. From the time a crust formed on the cooling earth about 5 billion years ago through the time life became complex enough to leave clear fossils; while simple spineless creatures developed into fish and crawled out onto land; during the eons insects and reptiles evolved and dinosaurs came to rule the earth — most of the land that is now Washington rose and fell again and again beneath the sea.

Some of the high, rugged peaks of the North Cascades are sediments from the floors of these ancient seas. A shell-strewn seabed perhaps 250 million years old, for example, became the limestone of subalpine Cave Ridge, north of Snoqualmie Pass, with its strange sinkholes and dangerous caves. A seabed that may be even older formed the limestone cliffs, columns, and sinkholes on Washington Monument, south of Mount Baker.

A limestone outcropping on Dock Butte, with Mount Baker in the distance.

How do these ancient sea floors come to stand bare on mountaintops? The theory most popular among geologists today for explaining volcanoes, earthquakes, the rise of mountains, and other great disturbances within the earth is that of continental drift and plate tectonics. According to this theory, the continents and ocean floors are pieces of a thin crust covering the earth. They shift like floating plates over a thicker layer of rock called the mantle. The movement of the plates is caused by hot spots in the earth where the crust is thin and magma rises, or the plates may be dragged into trenches by the sinking, cooling, heavier margin of the plate. As they have moved, the plates of the earth's crust have clashed, buckled, or overriden one another. These clashes push up mountains, shake the earth, and release the lava of volcanoes, according to the theory.

Ridges of the Pasayten Wilderness Area extend northward from Slate Peak.

About 300 million years ago, when reptiles were evolving, or at 10:30 P.M. if the earth's history were a twenty-four-hour day, most of the earth's dry land may have been grouped into two massive continents that lay close together. During the age of reptiles, these continents split and began to move toward their present positions. A theory for the Pacific Northwest holds that North America, pushed westward by the widening of the Atlantic Ocean floor, has overridden part of the Pacific Ocean floor. Following this theory, the collision between North America and the Pacific floor resulted in the formation of the Cascades, the Olympics, and the remaining skeleton of mountains, volcanoes, and earthquake faults bordering the eastern Pacific Ocean.

Rock formations show that, toward the end of the age of dinosaurs, the earth's mountain-building forces were active in part of what is now the Cascades. Sea floor sediments were laid down, later to become the ridges and valleys of the western Pasayten Wilderness of the northeastern Cascades. Still later the area that is today's North Cascades was lifted above the sea. Great sheets of rock that now form part of Mount Shuksan and some of its neighbors slid or were pushed up to thirty miles from their original bases.

About this time — some 80 million years ago or about 11:36 P.M. if the earth's history were a day — great masses of granite and granitelike rock began to be pushed up into the earth's crust from far beneath what is now the Cascades. One of the oldest of these intrusions now towers above the surrounding peaks as dark gray Mount Stuart. Bordering Mount Stuart to the south are rocks that may be still older: greenish, black-flecked serpentines that weather to rust color. Almost wherever they are found, these strange rocks, which may have escaped from the earth's deep mantle, crumble to make alien soils poisonous to many plants. (Apparently, this is because they are poor in calcium and rich in such minerals as nickel and chromium.) The gray green and rust red peaks south of Mount Stuart are streaked with "serpentine barrens" where little vegetation grows. Here plants appear in odd combinations or as strange subspecies found almost nowhere else.

Granitelike intrusions much younger than Mount Stuart's are exposed in the Cascades — for example, the Snoqualmie batholith, its gray granodiorite exposed on the mountainsides just north of the Snoqualmie Pass Highway (Interstate 90) and west of Snoqualmie Pass. This intrusion may be only 15 to 20 million years old, compared to Mount Stuart's 70 to 90 million years. In fact, new granitelike rocks may be being pushed into place far below the Cascades even now.

One result of the intrusions of long ago was the gold and silver rushes that marked the white man's conquest of the Cascades. Valuable ores are far more likely to form under conditions of vast heat and pressure as this rock is pushed into place far below the surface than when it pours onto the earth's surface as lava. Thus, the Cascades' old mines and gold rush districts are practically all found north of Snoqualmie Pass, where there are many such intrusions, and seldom south of the pass, where mountains are mostly capped with lava.

Mount Stuart, composed of granite, is the second highest nonvolcanic peak in Washington.

Leaf fossils found on the side of Church Mountain in the northern Cascades.

By 55 million years ago, after mammals and birds had begun to inhabit the land, those mountains formed in the age of dinosaurs were probably worn down to hills. A warm, wet climate produced masses of plants. As they died but did not fully decay, these plants formed coal beds at Chehalis, Renton, Issaquah, Bellingham, Cle Elum, Roslyn. Coal was later to power the first locomotives across the Cascades, to heat settlers' homes, and to give the pioneers fleeting dreams of a great iron industry.

Other kinds of sediments were deposited during this period when the seacoast lay east of its present location and much of today's mountain range was lake or swamp. Mud became shale; sand became sandstone; mixtures of mud and sand became rocks with characteristics between the two types. Although the Cascades have been changed too much by subsequent heating and folding to be good fossil-hunting country, many of the fossil leaves and shells found in the foothills were formed during this swampy period. In what are now the South Cascades, volcanoes sometimes erupted underwater, sometimes on dry land.

About 25 to 40 million years ago, around 11:50 P.M. if the earth's history were a day, a range of mountains rose with ridges and valleys running southeast-northwest. Examination of a map of today's Cascades shows that most of the big rivers flow out of the peaks in a southeast or northwest direction, still following the drainage patterns of this ancient range. In the South Cascades during this time, volcanoes rose whose eroded remnants are dramatic formations today: Stevens Ridge near Mount Rainier and pinnacled Fifes Peak farther east.

Rhinos, horses, and camels wandered about Washington when the state's next great geological stage began. About 15 million years ago, or 11:55 P.M. if the earth's history were a day, flow after flow of lava began to issue quietly from cracks in the earth in what is now southeastern Washington. Layer after layer of water-thin, quick-flowing, dark-colored lava called Columbia River basalt eventually formed a plain, covering more than 20,000 square miles of southeastern and southwestern Washington, crossing today's Cascades. Between flows, shallow lakes formed, forests grew, and animals flourished. Hunks of petrified wood found in the Cascades' southeastern foothills are remnants of such forests, buried by lava and now exposed again by erosion. Agates, chalcedony, and other beautiful stones, now sought by rockhounds, formed in gas bubbles in the lava. Sometimes found in stream gravels today they are most common downstream where the jostling current has ground softer rocks away.

The separate layers of different basalt flows from this period can be seen where rivers have cut canyons in the southeastern Cascades. As the basalt cooled and shrank, it sometimes formed rocks shattered into giant child's blocks covering a hillside or left black cliffs of vertical, often six-sided columns, packed next to one another like giant matchsticks, later stained with orange and chartreuse lichens. Parts of the wall of the Columbia Gorge and the canyons of the Cowlitz and Yakima are dramatic examples.

The Columbia basalt flows stopped less than 10 million years ago — 11:57 P.M. on our imaginary clock of the earth's history. By that time, most of southern Washington was a nearly flat lava plain. At this same time, the Pacific shore was near its present location. Puget Sound did not exist, but the land where it someday would be was already low in elevation. The old southeast-northwest range was probably worn to hills, and the stage was set for building today's mountains.

Basalt columns along the White Pass Highway.

The Mountains Rise

The 6 or 7 million years that have passed since the Cascades began to rise are less than .2 percent of the earth's 5-billion-year lifetime. This is a young age for a mountain range. In fact, some or all of these mountains may still be rising.

The Cascades rose, a massive arch that grew higher at its northern end. (The Washington Cascades' average height is nearly 8,000 feet near the Canadian border, but only about 3,500 feet near Oregon.) Roots of old mountains, debris of old volcanoes, ancient bottoms of rivers and seas, and masses of old and new granitelike rock were thrust upwards, much of it folded together and changed by heat and pressure from earlier disturbances in the earth. The result was a jumble of cracks, arches, and folds. Some are plainly visible — for example, the rainbowlike arch in layers of lava exposed on the wall of the Columbia Gorge.

The Cascades grew slowly — so slowly that some rivers carved their canyons faster than the mountains rose and thus kept their courses through them. This is how the Columbia maintained its course through the range, slowly carving the gorge that later became a main route for Indians and pioneers through the Cascade "wall." If you drive the scenic canyon road between Yakima and Ellensburg, you can see how the Yakima River kept the meandering course it had followed across a flat lava plain by wearing down a sinuous canyon through the surrounding hills.

Prusik Peak rises above Gnome Tarn in the Enchantment Lakes region.

Mount Saint Helens displays the symmetry of its eastern slopes.

Fire from the Earth

When the great ice sheets began to retreat from Washington about 14,000 years ago, the Cascades were shaped much as they are today. Major valleys, lakes, and passes had been cut. Ice and time had made ruins of old volcanoes, like the one whose remains are the crags and pinnacles of Goat Rocks Wilderness Area, south of White Pass in the South Cascades.

As the Ice Age drew to a close, the five volcanoes that now tower above Washington's Cascades were still taking on their shapes. Although the rest of today's Cascades began rising 6 or 7 million years ago, Mount Baker, Glacier Peak, Mount Rainier, Mount Adams, and Mount Saint Helens in their present forms are probably less than a million years old. Some of these giants have erupted within man's memory, and they sleep only fitfully. Scientists watch them closely, knowing that Rainier, Baker, and Saint Helens, in particular, could erupt at any time.

There are many kinds of volcanic eruptions. Where thin lava pours quietly out of the earth, a volcano may form into a low but immensely broad cone called a shield volcano. Indian Heaven, the gentle area between Mount Adams and Mount Saint Helens where Indians gathered to harvest berries, covers the remains of old shield volcanoes. Red Mountain, at the south end of Indian Heaven, is a shield volcano that may have covered twenty square miles.

The five towering volcanoes of the Washington Cascades, however, are stratovolcanoes, also called composite volcanoes. Many eruptions of different kinds, often from several vents, gradually built their cones. You can read some of this complex geological history as you hike the slopes today.

Tonguelike ridges, cracked into huge blocks or covered with soil and trees, may be old flows of thick lava. Perhaps the most striking examples are the Big Lava Beds, an area nine miles long and up to four miles across, between Mount Adams and Mount Saint Helens. The tonguelike flows that poured from a vent near the area's north end are so young that they are scarcely eroded. Their thin soil supports only scrubby forests. In this broken moonscape, a walk up a grassy slope may end suddenly at a sheer well or at a topless tube thirty feet deep or more. These wells and tubes were formed when the exterior of a lava flow cooled to solid rock, while the still-molten lava inside flowed on or was blown out by gas. There was plenty of time for this to happen. As you can see in the rough, pitted case that edges many glassy volcanic bounders, gas bubbles rose to the edge of the cooling lava. This foamy exterior was excellent insulation that could keep the inside of a thirty-foot-high lava flow hot for three years or more.

Lava tube caves and pits — explained by Indians as the tunnelings of a jealous giant — honeycomb the forests between Mount Adams and Mount Saint Helens. Ape Cave, south of Mount Saint Helens, is more than two miles long — the longest lava tube cave yet found in the United States. Settlers made use of the tubes' cool, steady temperatures. They stored butter in Butter Cave, meat in Meat Cave, and hacked ice from Ice Cave to supply the town of Hood River, Oregon. Ice Cave and Ape Cave are in Forest Service picnic areas today and are easy to visit. Other caves and wells sit neglected beside back roads. Exploring is not advised: crumbling rock and sudden drop-offs make some of them extremely dangerous.

Not all eruptions flowed like those that left behind the shield volcanoes and the lava tongues. Some exploded. Occasionally you may find rounded rocks on a volcano's slopes that look like what they are called — volcanic bombs. These globs of lava were hurled into the air like lumps of tar, hardening into round or teardrop shapes later.

At other times, volcanoes spewed glowing clouds of gas and volcanic "cinders" — rock ground in the volcano's crater or powdered by rapid expansion of gas in the explosive eruption. Clouds from these eruptions darkened the sky and covered the earth for miles around. Geologists date many events from the foot-thick layer of ash that covered much of northern and eastern Washington after Glacier Peak's last big eruption 12,000 years ago.

Volcanic cinders also form small, neat cones, rarely more than 1,000 feet high, around many volcanic vents in the South Cascades. Because loose cinders erode easily, these cones are usually signs of fairly recent eruptions. Potato Hill, a nearly perfect cinder cone and crater on the north side of Mount Adams, and Little Mount Adams on the south side are evidence of eruptions through the side of the big volcano.

In other explosive eruptions, gas bubbles expanding within the liquid rock formed pumice — frothy glass that you can crumble in your hand, and that will float if thrown into water. Pumice from eruptions only a few hundred years old litters many of the upper slopes of Mount Saint Helens.

Another kind of volcanic formation, the neck or chimney, which resembles its name, is composed of hard lava that solidified inside a vent and then withstood the erosion of the cone around it. The crumbled black outcrop called Goat Rock, on the north side of Mount Saint Helens, is one example of this kind of formation.

Combine the volcanoes' complex origins with the very different effects that erosion has had on each, and it is not surprising that each of the big volcanoes has a distinctive "character." Their dispositions differ in yet another way: some seem to be growing calmer and cooler, while others are more likely to erupt dangerously.

Ice Cave near Trout Lake, south of Mount Adams – a source of ice for early settlers.

Clouds of steam boil out of Mount Baker's Sherman Crater.

Mount Baker, northernmost of the Washington Cascade volcanoes, is the most active of the five today. Heat and fumes have long maintained steam caves and sent down occasional avalanches from its main cone. In 1975, this steaming suddenly increased, accompanied by sulfurous fumes from the newer of its main vents. Scientists have kept a close watch on the mountain since. Their main fear is that the heating-up of the mountain could cause a flow of melted snow and loose rock that would bring floods to the lakes and valleys below.

By contrast, 10,658-foot Glacier Peak, the next volcano south, has been the quietest of Cascade volcanoes in recent history. It seems to have calmed down abruptly since an explosion of 12,000 years ago spread ash across the country. Hot springs like popular Kennedy Hot Springs are almost its only sign of activity today.

Aerial view of Mount Rainier. Nisqually Glacier flows to the left and Emmons Glacier to the right.

Mount Rainier, at 14,410 feet the tallest of Cascade volcanoes, once towered at least 1,000 feet higher. Little Tahoma, the bump on the mountain's east flank that Indian legend called Mount Rainier's son, is a remnant of this original cone. Much of it was probably carried away in mudflows like one 5,700 years ago, which covered sixty-five miles, as far as the present site of Kent. Later eruptions built two small craters atop Rainier's collapsed summit. Scientists who watch Rainier's changing lakes and steam caves amid the ice say that here, as on Mount Baker, the biggest threat is another flow of water and rock turned to mud by volcanic heat and fumes.

Massive Mount Adams with Potato Hill, a cinder cone, in the foreground.

The blunt head of Mount Adams, in Indian legend flattened by a battle with Mount Hood, seems to be the result of eruptions from several vents near the summit. Scarcely eroded cinder cones and recent vents on Adams' sides and base show the complex building of this volcano which continued well after the Ice Age. Today, though steam and odorous hydrogen sulfide gas still seep from its icy summit, the mountain seems to be cooling off. At 12,307 feet it is second to Rainier in height.

Mount Saint Helens is the lowest of the five volcanoes, at 9,677 feet. It also is the youngest, although its present cone rests on the roots of a much older volcano. A sign of this youth is the symmetrical cone of Saint Helens, scarcely touched by ice cutting — the cone that made the mountain a beautiful woman in Indian legend. Not only has its cone largely been built since the end of the Ice Age; its present summit probably is only a few hundred years old. Other signs of recent eruptions are the volcano's unusually low timberline — only about 4,400 feet, compared to 6,900 feet on Mount Rainier farther north — and the few meadows on the high mountainside. Lava apparently has not had time to decay into soil to support plants. Several times between 1842 and 1857, Mount Saint Helens sent forth spectacular eruptions of steam, ashes, and lava. A Methodist minister who was seventy-five miles away in Oregon described the 1842 eruption this way:

> Where Mt. St. Helens should have been there were only clouds of smoke and steam. The base was of very black smoke that spread out for an immense distance, involving all the northern horizon; above it grew lighter in color, culminating in vast columns and wreaths of white steam, that penetrated the zenith .... White puffs of steam rose like columns of scroll work to the very mid-heavens, constantly changing and assuming new forms upon the sky .... Ashes and rocks were thrown out with tremendous force, but no noise was heard at that distance .... Flames were seen for a long time issuing from a crater on the south side of the mountain .... Ashes fell all over the country from the Dalles to the Pacific Ocean.

An eruption of this young and possibly still-growing volcano is likely to be deadly: experts warn that a mudflow could cause disastrous floods in the reservoirs along the Lewis River.

Scientists are not certain any of the Cascade volcanoes will erupt; however, geologically, all of them are youthful.

The Chiselers

Although glaciers, volcanoes, rivers, and huge movements of the earth's crust are the great sculptors of the Cascades, more subtle natural forces also scratch and pick at the rocks. Forest fire, frost, flood, wind, plant roots, burrowing animals, chemical reactions of rainwater and rotting plants — even the day-night cycle of heat and cold — all work to gnaw away the peaks. Erosion aids erosion: as heavy layers of rock are eaten away, the release of pressure lets rock beneath expand, opening up cracks that hasten a mountain's destruction.

Guessing the cause of the ruins every high-country traveler sees develops an understanding of a huge peak's life and death. The rounded boulder by your campfire was probably polished by a glacier, or perhaps in a stream. Or it may have "exfoliated" — a process whereby bits of rock flake off because of release of pressure on the rock or weakening of mineral bonds within the rock. This bit-by-bit, onionskin-type peeling can round off, then flatten the top of a half-buried, jagged boulder, shaping a rock that makes a good table for your lunch on a hike. On a grander scale, exfoliation can make stone mountaintops rounded and polished like bald heads.

A majestic ice carving – McAllister Glacier and its knifelike ridges. Glacier Peak is seen in the distant center and Eldorado Peak to the right.

Frost-chipped rocks form the summit of Magic Mountain in North Cascades National Park.

Layered rocks — whether made of soft sediment, like shale, or hard minerals separated by heat and pressure, like schist — tend to crack along their layers. Prying frost will make jagged, angular rocks, from tiny chips to pinnacled peaks. Water also works its way into invisible cracks where it freezes and pries the rock loose. Screes or taluses — those slopes of loose, angular rock where you slide down one step for every two you take up — are likely to have been produced by frost chipping at the mountain above.

Frost can also arrange large and small rocks into stripes and polygons in loose soil. Ice, forming lenses or strips along drainage lines, pushes larger pebbles away. You will see this "patterned ground" from time to time in the high Cascades.

Snow and its meltwater may have gentling effects: they can work to form meadows. Snow lingering at the shady back of a hollow can hasten breakdown of the rock there. Runoff and snowslides on watersoaked earth carry dirt and rock forward to the front of the hollow. This slow work can lengthen the "tread" of a flat. Eventually it can build a meadow. Some of the flowery alpine and subalpine meadows of the Cascades were probably built by this gentle snow erosion.

A carpet of avalanche lilies in Spray Park, Mount Rainier National Park.

A Walk Through Seasons and Worlds

On a sunny summer day, the cherries have already been harvested from orchards on the southeastern edge of the Cascades near Yakima. The foothills of crumbled lava, where the Naches and Tieton rivers pour out of the mountains, are brown and dry, hung with fragrant white lace of traveler's joy and mock orange. Rimrock Lake, an irrigation reservoir in a canyon of pinkish lava, is bright blue and brimful of melted snow. Motorboats zigzag like waterbugs on its surface. Paved and dirt roads rim the lake, wandering through miles of pine and Douglas fir with grassy open spaces between the trees.

The road along the South Fork of the Tieton River ends at a long meadow that continues upriver. Here the grass is not brown, but fresh and green. In some spots, the meadow is almost blue with larkspur and lupine. The windings of a small stream through the meadow are marked by tropical-looking Indian hellebore, already four feet tall, with broad foot-long leaves curving out from its stems.

The river, with its border of tall conifers, sometimes meanders near the trail. At a log crossing there is a swampy spot with fragrant white bog orchid (an Indian good-luck charm) and odd-looking, partly parasitic elephant head, its foot-tall spikes sporting pink purple flowers with trunks and tusks. On a sandy flat a foot or two higher blooms another beautiful curiosity: mariposa lily, its three white petals drawing to a hair-lined, golden throat.

At the end of the meadow, the trail switches up a steep slope thick with Douglas fir. Only a few white flowers bloom in the evergreen shade. You are cooled on the hot climb by the sound of a stream plunging almost straight down the mountain along a narrow, boulder-lined groove.

Suddenly the trail levels out, and in a few more steps you are looking down into Surprise Lake. Trees grow to the water line in this steep-sided bowl. At its northern end, the lake narrows into a small feeder stream. A little farther north along this creek, the trees open onto a shelf of meadows still dotted with July's remaining snow patches. Here the trees huddle together in rows and clumps; true firs begin to replace the Douglas firs of lower levels.

Glacier lilies burst through August snow patches.

The flowers of early mountain spring are in bloom in this high meadow. Hollows are filled with avalanche lilies, their white petals curved back to display golden centers. Marsh marigolds with shiny scalloped leaves nod where the ground is soaked with melted snow. Above, the pinnacles of Goat Rocks and the Devil's Horns are still wrapped in winter. Spring will not arrive there, where only a few hardy plants cling above treeline, for another month.

This day's hike has brought you through some of the mountains' many worlds. These worlds are divided partly by location: how high they are on the mountain, whether they face north, south, east, or west. They are also divided by weather, by water, by the kind of soil, and by human history — whether the area was grazed, burned, logged, or flooded.

A chart on page 41 divides the Cascades into a very broad set of communities or zones. It is based on the "climax" vegetation of each area, that is, the species that would eventually dominate a zone more or less permanently if nature took its course without interference from ice ages, climate changes, or man.

Generalized Vegetation Map of Washington – from **Vegetation of Oregon and Washington** *by Jerry F. Franklin and C.T. Dyrness, U.S.D.A. Forest Service Research Paper PNW-80, 1969. Used by permission of U.S. Forest Service.*

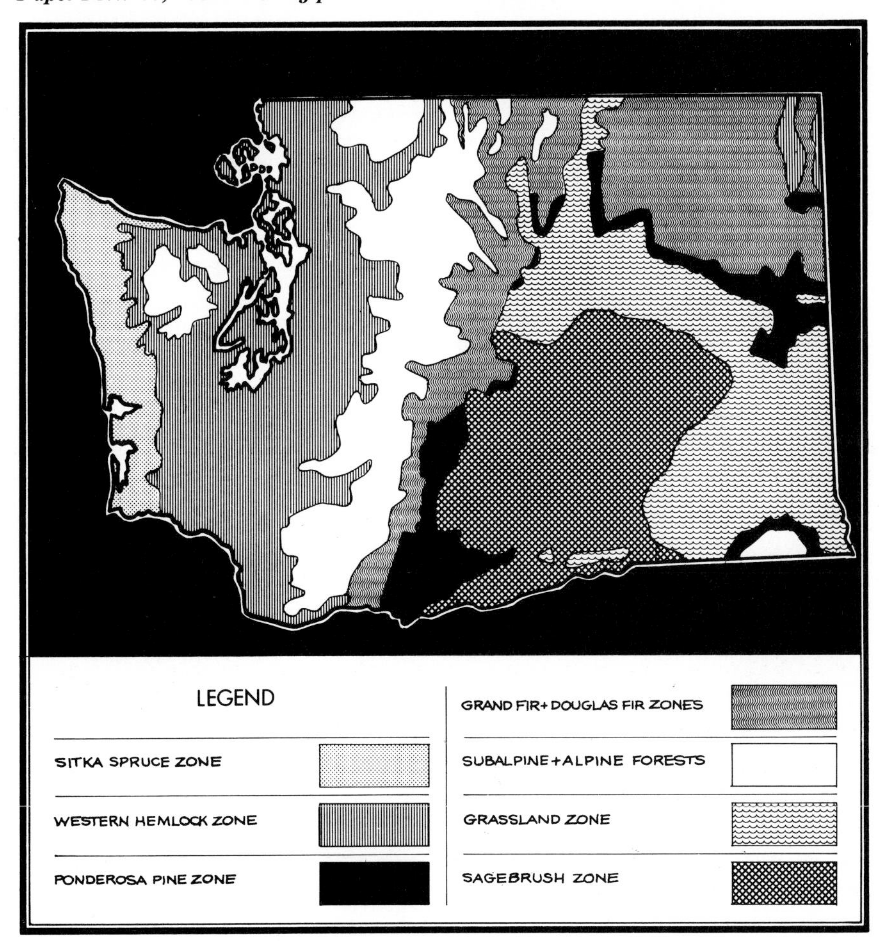

Dragontail Peak in the Enchantment Peaks region.
Lichens and mosses will be the first vegetation to inhabit these barren slopes.

At High Altitudes: Alpine and Subalpine Life

Even on the Cascades' frozen peaks, there is life. In areas where snow and ice endure, one-celled algae bloom when snowbanks soften in spring. A common variety, growing thickly, forms the patches of pink or red snow that mountain travelers often see. Millions of worms infest the dirt, ice, and snow of the Cascade glaciers. Pollen, blown onto the glaciers, feeds insects called springtails, while a daddy-longlegs-like spider preys on these hopping "glacier fleas." The upslope mountain winds carry seeds and insects as well as pollen onto the icy surface. A few birds, like the little rosy finch that summers in the high Cascades, walk about on the snow and ice, feeding on the wind's harvest.

At the edges of permanent glaciers and snowfields, mountains often crumble into boulders, rock chips, and gravel, forming heaped moraines or sliding away steeply as scree slopes. Strong winds whip at the knife-edged ridges. Water drains away quickly through the loose rock; rockslides and heaving frost combine to tear plants from their roots. It seems a barren, unfriendly world indeed.

Surprisingly, life does creep into this chilly desert. Rocks are stained with what look like orange scales, curly, gray papery growths, or pads of crumbly, dark brown moss. Green tufts, looking like little pincushions, cling to crannies, terraces, and rockslides, waving bright flowers in the short summer. These plants are pioneers. Special characteristics help them survive in a tougher world than that of their lowland relatives.

The powdery scales on rocks — dry growths like dead leaves, curled wigs, or tiny frosted trees — are lichens. These are really two plants: a partnership between a fungus and an alga. The fungus — the scaly, leafy, or branching growth you see — shields the alga inside or beneath it from light and drying. The alga, in turn, manufactures food that feeds the fungus. Lichens can survive long dry spells that would kill so-called "higher" plants. They simply dry out and wait. (Of course, these plants live lower in the Cascades, too. They hang in black beards or chartreuse curls from pine branches and cover rotting trunks with gray scales.)

Mosses, also pioneers, are most common in the Cascades' low, wet forests. Some kinds, however, play a special role in the high, cold desert of the peaks. Because they do not depend upon roots for nourishment the way "higher" plants do, mosses can survive on bare rock or on soil where slides and frost heaving would tear ordinary plants from their roots. They do have shallow, rootlike structures that serve as anchors and absorb water; their leaflike green parts also absorb water and nutrients.

In dry times, the moss cushions on these high-mountain rocks curl their leaves to show hard brown backs that slow evaporation. They look black and dead. When water finally comes, they absorb it quickly. In seconds, the apple green leaves unfurl to catch every drop of available moisture. Almost at once the moss turns green and velvety again. No flowering plant could perform this magic.

The velvety piles of high-mountain mosses also trap dust that builds soil for other plants. Eventually, this dust combines with rotting mosses, lichens, and decayed rocks to build a thin, rocky soil that can support more complex plants.

Dewdrops on the hairy leaves of subalpine lupine.

Gardens above the Trees

You can see these pioneer plant communities, alpine rock gardens, on almost any hike above timberline in the Cascades; in general, the white areas on U.S. Geological Survey contour maps show where to find them.

An alpine rock garden often sports a welter of color in the late mountain spring — mosses, lichens, yellow stonecrop, blue lupine, white partridge-foot, pink phlox, and rosy pussy's toes. These plants are surprisingly similar — low, with leaves bunched in rosettes, mats, or pincushions. Most have hairy, gray green leaves or waxy, fleshy ones, like desert plants.

By lying low, these plants avoid the worst of the peak's cold, drying winds. In winter, they are insulated by a blanket of snow, while the temperature above may be twenty degrees below zero Fahrenheit.

Some plants, with leaves bunched into rosettes and pincushions like the saxifrages, or fringed like those of yarrow or partridge-foot, retain a bit of still air, warmth, and moisture in the small, sheltered spaces among their leaves. The temperature inside one of these alpine cushions may be several degrees warmer than outside — perhaps the critical difference between life and death. Hairy leaves, like those of pussy's toes, reduce water loss by slowing the wind and helping hold a thin layer of moist air around the leaf. Succulent fleshy leaves, like those of stonecrop, store water, and waxy leaf coatings help retain it.

The Cascades' flowering alpine pioneers also have features in common that are not so easy to see. Their root systems seem huge when compared with those of many lowland plants. A tuft of furry *Eriogonum,* less than an inch high, may have a taproot as thick as your finger and longer. Such roots help hold these plants against slides and frost heaving. They also help locate nutrients and moisture in the crumble of rock and dust.

Most alpine plants are perennials, springing from the same roots year after year. Any plant species would have a hard time in these hostile rock fields if it died each fall and survival depended on a seed finding a new habitable cranny. Some plants, like the common rock cress, include annual or biennial varieties that flourish at low altitudes and perennial varieties that live on the peaks.

Many of the alpine dwarfs reproduce without seed — for example, by underground runners with growing buds protected from the cold, drying air. Since pollinizing insects may not be drawn to the bare, rocky high-mountain gardens, some alpine plants can produce fertile seed without fertilization, a talent less common in their lowland relatives.

In fact, some of the tiny plants that flourish at high altitudes are like mutant superplants. They are "diploid" or "polyploid," which means they have double, triple, or even quadruple the number of genes of their lowland kin. Polyploid species are often able to survive cold, drought, and other extremes better than their "normal" relatives.

High altitude trees on Denny Mountain have short limbs that will not break off with snow. Mount Rainier is in the distance.

Trees and Meadows

High on the rocky slopes the first trees appear, dwarfed and twisted like hunched, shriveled old men. This is the "elfin forest." Its firs, spruces, hemlocks, and cedars may be hundreds of years old, but cold temperatures and winds carrying knife-edged ice crystals prevent them from ever growing as tall as those living in the lowlands. Lift the limbs of one of these dense evergreen mounds, and you may find it sheltering a tiny meadow of fresh green plants that otherwise could only survive much lower on the mountain. Mats of evergreen shrubs also survive in these high rock fields: pungent juniper in dry spots, or low tangles of heather hung with red and white bells in spring.

As conditions grow gentler lower on the mountains, trunks survive above the snow. At first they rise only a few feet. Sparse limbs and few needles contrast sharply with the bushy mat below winter's snow level. Often these trees are limbless where snowslides and icy winds have bombarded them — or they are bent away from these attackers.

Where nature is still milder, spruce, fir, and hemlock take the shape of subalpine trees on picture postcards: dense, symmetrical conical forms, with branches to the ground. They grow in clumps scattered artistically about meadows, in sheltered spots, or strung across lips and ledges. These subalpine evergreen trees of the Cascades are as carefully adapted as alpine wildflowers to the high, cold mountain "desert." Needlelike leaves help them survive winter's "drought" when they cannot draw moisture from the frozen ground. The needles' small area reduces evaporation. (Heather and crowberry, evergreen shrubs of alpine meadows, have similar needlelike leaves.) A stiff, waxy coating, lending these high-mountain conifers a silver blue sheen, also reduces water loss from the leaves. The dense cone shape of subalpine fir trees sheds snow like a steep roof. Although subalpine larch and whitebark pine grow in looser shapes, they have strong, almost rubbery limbs that bend and do not break under strong wind and heavy snow.

In spite of such adaptations, trees must struggle to get a toehold in the high peaks. The "landscaping" of the high Cascades into parklike meadows and clumps of trees is the landscaping of necessity. Conifer clumps rise only in favorable spots: perhaps on sunny south-facing slopes, or on a rise where snow melts early. The trees provide warmth and shelter for one another — one reason they grow in their artistic groupings. In early spring, a hollow will form where the snow has melted around the base of a tree trunk, demonstrating the warmth absorbed and given off by the tree's dark bark and foliage. The wealth of plants flourishing under some of these tree clumps is another sign of the tiny milder climate the trees provide.

Parklike Horseshoe Basin in the Pasayten Wilderness Area.

The tree species that gains a toehold provides a clue to conditions in the high Cascades. Subalpine fir, whitebark pine, and especially juniper survive dryness well. Subalpine fir seems to be the main "climax" species on the Cascades' high eastern slopes. Mountain hemlock and Engelmann spruce are more moisture-loving. Mountain hemlock seems to be the dominant subalpine species on the western slopes. Subalpine larch or tamarack, spreads its pale green veil mainly on the northernmost Cascades, in places like the Pasayten Wilderness. It brightens to gold in fall and loses its needles in winter — perhaps as an added protection against winter's frozen drought.

In these parklike subalpine meadows throughout the Cascades, distinctive types of ground covers also signal conditions of soil and climate. The swampiest and driest are often grassy — fresh green in spring, golden in fall. Others, with moderate moisture levels, are composed of ankle-high tangles of heather, or dwarf huckleberry, crimson in fall when its leaves turn color. Some areas, moist but well drained, begin a yearly flower show with avalanche lilies, buttercups, white marsh marigolds, anemones, or globe flowers nodding by melting snowbanks. Later, delicate valerian perfumes the air, and bistort waves its little white brushes. The show runs into September with yellow arnica, purple aster, blue gentian, scarlet paintbrush.

Elephant's-head, an attractive member of the figwort family, grows in the high meadows of the Cascade Range.

The attracting colors, scents, and shapes of many of these high-meadow flowers encourage a fleeting partnership with insects. The lower petals of trumpet-shaped flowers serve as landing platforms for bees. Some, like pentstemon, even have dark lines called "honey guides," which help lead bees to the flower's nectar. Larkspur and other flowers with long spurs aim at forcing insects to crawl deep into the flower to get the nectar in the spur, thereby rubbing pollen on their furry bodies. Beetles crawling into flower cups and even the biting black flies that no hiker can love help pollinate the flowers. Flies catch and carry pollen when they suck on wide-open flowers like buttercups, whose centers can be punctured by the fly's short, piercing proboscis.

"Fragile" is a word often used to describe these alpine and subalpine meadows — and they are. It took thousands of years for soil to gather and be seized by these plants' matted roots. Cut a trail in the root mat, and rivers of melting snow can make it an ugly scar many times its original size. Heavy boots can kill a wildflower just by packing the soil around its roots. Even weight on the protective blanket of winter snow can transform the snow into ice that smothers the plants beneath. Once damaged, the slow-spreading alpine and subalpine perennials may take generations to fight their way back against the harsh forces of weather and erosion.

High-Mountain Dwellers

Subalpine meadows hum, chatter, and squeak with life as you walk into a high meadow on a sunny day. There is a steady buzz of bees around your feet. Blue or brown butterflies drink on the muddy trail ahead of you, slowly opening and closing their wings. A marmot whistles or a pika squeaks in alarm from the rock field edging the meadow. A chipmunk or a ground squirrel scurries to his burrow under a rock or log.

Small birds with tinkling calls forage from tree to tree. A flicker flashes red underwings as it darts from one snag to another, "woodpecking" for food. Clark's nutcrackers warn one another of your arrival with raucous caws. Out over the valley, a pair of red-tailed hawks circle on the upslope winds. The sun makes a reddish halo of their translucent tip feathers.

If you are lucky, you may sight mountain goats making an unhurried exit up the valley walls. Still more rarely, perhaps at dawn, you may see a fox trotting along or a weasel with its humpbacked gait sniffing about on its hunting circuit.

The creatures of the peaks divide up and use just about every resource the high mountain offers — every kind of shelter and every food, including one another. Take as an example the little mammals that depend on the plants of high, rock-edged meadows: marmots, pikas, ground squirrels, yellow pine chipmunks, mice, pocket gophers. Their signs are everywhere: pikas' haystacks drying outside burrows; earth cores and mounds tossed up by tunneling pocket gophers; stripped cones; packed-earth highways leading to holes half-hidden under rocks or logs.

These animals eat almost everything the high mountain produces. Conifer seeds, huckleberries, juniper berries, crowberries, lily bulbs, aster, grass, lupine seeds, pentstemon, sorrel, mountain dandelion shoots, manzanita berries, saxifrage, stonecrop, lichens, mushrooms, ants, grasshoppers, bird eggs and young birds comprise only a portion of nature's bounty. Although some animals may like many of the same delicacies, they manage to divide the harvest, live in the same meadows, share the same network of trails, and even nest in the same rockslides in relative peace.

Such harmony does not occur from a lack of fighting spirit, however. Even to their own kind, these animals can be fierce. Male ground squirrels attack and sometimes injure their young. (This probably serves to drive the young to new areas.) Pocket gophers defend their tunnel systems from other pocket gophers. Watch a colony of pikas on a rockslide, and you will find that individuals spend much of their time squeaking over possession of territories and chasing other pikas away.

A marmot nibbles on lupine in high mountain meadows.

These different species can share the same area because of slightly different habits. Pikas and marmots gather food in the sunlight, while the large-footed meadow mouse seeks the same food at night (as many a camper has found when his sleep was shattered by mysterious rustlings). The meadow mouse also has an alternate food source that the pikas and marmots do not exploit; in addition to feeding on seeds, bulbs, stems, and leaves, the meadow mouse can swim and dive in mountain pools for insects and larvae.

Pikas and marmots sometimes live in the same piles of mountain rock. However, the little rabbitlike pikas don't hibernate; they dry needles, grass, and seeds in haystacks for winter use. Marmots do hibernate, and in preparation, eat large quantities of summer seeds and greens to fatten themselves for a long winter sleep. They seem to venture farther from their dens to gather food than do pikas.

In the same way, chipmunks and ground squirrels burrow under logs or rocks and eat many of the same foods. But the yellow pine chipmunk of subalpine meadows also climbs low trees and bushes to gather food that the golden-mantled ground squirrel waits to take after it falls to the ground.

The shapes and markings of high-mountain mammals provide clues to their survival. A rounded body helps an animal adapt to greater cold, for example. Short legs, ears, and tails help prevent loss of body heat — for instance, the little short-eared pika that inhabits the coldest alpine and subalpine heights. At lower elevations live its relatives — rabbits and hares, with long, erect ears, longer legs, and projecting tails.

Yellow pine chipmunks and golden-mantled ground squirrels are studies in camouflage, although their bright yellow coats with strong white and dark stripes may not seem so at first. These markings help them blend into the background by breaking up outlines and disguising distinctive features. A dark stripe through the chipmunk's eye probably makes it harder to spot the shiny bead of an eyeball that would give away its presence. Paler-colored underparts provide countershading when light falls on the ground squirrel's back and its underparts are in the shade. Patches of light and dark break up its outline against any background, helping it blend with the dappled light and shade in the forest.

Mountain goats may be seen picking their way calmly across cliffs in the high Cascades. (They tend to be shy, but you have a fair chance of spotting them in Mount Rainier National Park, a good chance if you take the boat up Lake Chelan in winter and look for them on the cliffs along the lake.) These smallish hoofed grazers — about three and one-half feet at the shoulder — are not true goats at all, but relatives of the chamois and other antelopes of Europe and Asia. Nor do they always cling to the mountaintops; sometimes they wander down into forests, particularly during bad weather when trees offer shelter.

For most of the year, nannies lead the bands of mothers and young, while billies lead bachelorlike lives apart from or on the outskirts of their little flocks. In autumn, billies begin courting the females with low crouching entreaties, often answered by the threatening horns of the female or by ritualized fights with other males. Their fights can be a bit of a sham: rivals may just sit on their haunches, side by side, each pawing the ground to indicate their anger. On rarer occasions, mountain goats *do* battle and seriously injure one another.

The mountain or bighorn sheep you may see in the high, dry, rocky eastern Cascades is a true sheep. When white men brought domestic sheep to summer in the mountains, bighorns were almost wiped out by scabies, a sheep disease. Hunters and competition for grazing land also took their tolls. Today only the mountain sheep of the extreme northeastern Cascades are likely to be natives. Washington's other herds come from reintroduced stock. (A few sheep wander from Canada into the Cascade Pass area, but your best chance of seeing them is on Mount Aeneas near Loomis, Okanogan County, on the extreme eastern edge of the range.)

Mountain sheep are not strictly high-mountain animals. They wander throughout rocky, near-desert foothills if they do not face too much disturbance by man or too much competition with other grazers.

A mountain goat surveys its kingdom near Alpine Lookout above Lake Wenatchee.

A high-mountain dweller – the golden-mantled ground squirrel.

If you have difficulty distinguishing the sheep from the goats, remember that mountain goats have long, shaggy fur once valued by the Indians for making blankets. They are pure white, except for black hooves, noses, and slightly curved horns. Mountain sheep, on the other hand, have grayish, fairly short coats. The horns of females and young males are merely back-pointing crescents, but those of males eventually grow to a full circular curl — hence the name bighorn sheep.

High-Mountain Birds – For Non-Bird Watchers

Only a few kinds of birds nest in the Cascades' highest stone fields and meadows: the white-tailed ptarmigan, the horned lark, the water pipit, the gray-crowned rosy finch, and some cliff-nesting swallows and swifts. These above-timberline birds are generally a mousy-colored crew. Dull gray, brown, and white feathers probably help hide such ground-nesting birds as the ptarmigan, the horned lark, and the water pipit from meat and egg predators.

These birds have other adaptations for survival in the high, bare peaks. The white-tailed ptarmigan, the only bird to stay in the high mountains throughout the year, changes its plumage to pure white during the snowy months. Its feathered legs, ending in large feet equipped with horny "snowshoes," help provide warmth and support on winter's soft snow. (Look for ptarmigans pecking about like small chickens near the snow's edge on Mount Rainier.)

Like the little mammals that forage in mountain meadows, the birds above timberline eat many of the same insects and seeds. Different habits reduce competition among them. The bobbing, jerking water pipit likes damp places and even wades for food. (Look for him near the shores of rocky lakes, such as the Enchantment Lakes near Leavenworth.) The horned lark seeks food on the ground, like the water pipit, but prefers to nest on drier spots in deserts as well as on mountaintops.

In subalpine meadows where tree clumps can survive, the number of bird species you are likely to see increases because there is more variety of habitat for them. In the dense evergreen forests lower down, as in the treeless meadows higher up, there is less varied habitat than in the subalpine parklands, and you can expect less varied animal life in these locations.

Learning to know birds takes a good pair of binoculars and a great deal of patience. There is much to be seen — and heard — even if you don't know the birds by name. Waking on a ridge in early summer, you will sometimes notice that the bird chorus of trills, twitters, chirps, harsh rattles, and nassal "yanks" is louder to the sunny east than on the shady west. Lying in your sleeping bag at first light, reluctant to face the chill, you can hear the birds begin with a few broken fragments, gradually working up to their full repertoires. Some stop singing before it is fully daylight. Sometimes your ears can follow birds such as woodpeckers while they move across a hillside, rattling their dawn announcement of territory.

Spring and early summer are bird courtship and breeding seasons and hence singing seasons. Most commonly, the male perches alone in a prominent spot and sings to attract and hold a mate and to repel other males from his chosen territory. This exclusive territory provides food and insures separation from rivals, predators, and disease.

A study in camouflage – the ptarmigan in winter and summer plumage.

As pairing season ends and the young go out on their own, you will see a change in most birds' habits. Singing decreases; territories are abandoned; many birds begin to gather and move in flocks. Flocks, like exclusive territories, may aid the birds in several ways: they discourage hawks and other enemies, make it easier to find food (when one member finds food, the others can follow). Towards fall the two-way migration begins. Some birds fly south for warmth. Hummingbirds of subalpine meadows may winter in Mexico. Others flee to lower altitudes. The robin in your backyard in winter may have nested in summer in a meadow near timberline.

The foraging flocks in the mountains in fall and winter seem constantly on the move. Like small mammals, small birds lose heat and energy quickly. In winter's mountain country, the search for food becomes a life-or-death matter that consumes nearly all the waking hours of the small birds that remain. To survive the night, they ruffle their feathers, take shelter in hollows, leafy plants, or behind bark, and sometimes huddle together. Some have the knack of lowering their body temperatures to reduce use of heat and energy. Even so, hard winters take a heavy toll of little birds like kinglets, wrens, and warblers.

Different bird species hunt in different ways. Mountain chickadees flutter from limb to limb and often hang upside-down. Mountain bluebirds fly, hover, and perch low, looking for insects on the ground. It is not hard to see that many birds are built for their tasks. Those that probe, like the hummingbird that sips from flower necks, and the creeper that hunts insects in cracks in bark, have long, narrow beaks. Swifts, swallows, and other birds that spend much of their time on the wing, scooping insects out of the air, often have short, wide beaks and small feet and legs.

The Clark's nutcracker, one of the birds most characteristic of subalpine areas in the Cascades, is built for its way of life with a unique adaptation: a pouch under its tongue that lets it carry food without swallowing it. This bird, looking like a small, light gray crow with white patches on black wings and tail, is a flock dweller that announces your arrival with harsh "kraws." If you watch it feed, you will see that its long, powerful beak can hammer at cones and pull off their scales to get to the seeds inside.

For years, the nutcracker's nesting habits were a mystery, for their flocks returned to their high-mountain nesting areas in March and early April — much earlier than other mountain birds, and so early that it seemed unlikely they could survive in the still-snowy land. It was eventually learned that nutcrackers have the unusual habit of storing food, chiefly conifer seeds, in caches each fall for their return in spring. They carry the seeds in the pouches under their tongues to the caches, which are often located in tree hollows.

In some ways, the Clark's nutcracker may be as important to the subalpine parklands as the land is to the bird. The nutcracker stores some of its seeds under a log, for instance, and some of these may be forgotten in the spring. The "planted" seeds have a better-than-average chance to sprout and spread the tree's seedlings beyond the spots where cones would naturally fall.

Great blue heron at a melt pond at 5,000 feet in the Glacier Peak Wilderness Area.

Clark's nutcracker is often seen in subalpine areas of the Cascades.

Mount Baker from Sauk Mountain.

At Lower Altitudes: Evergreen Forest Life

Ancient western red cedars in Big Beaver Valley, North Cascades Park.

At lower, less severe altitudes, the clumps of trees in subalpine parklands merge into true forests. Trees typical of lower altitudes mingle with the subalpine species; Douglas fir, western hemlock, grand fir, and Pacific silver fir become common. At still lower elevations, these evergreen giants rule the forest.

The Cascades contain some of the world's most magnificent evergreen forests — giants that at one time spread over much of the mountainous northwestern corner of North America. These huge cone-bearing trees, like biological relics, evolved before today's more common flowering plants. They once covered much more of the earth's surface. Today they seem to find refuge where conditions do not suit the modern flowering trees: in high mountains, cold climates, and relatively poor soils.

Old-growth trees may be more than 200 feet tall and more than ten feet in diameter. In North America, only the sequoias grow larger than Douglas firs and western red cedars. These evergreen giants mature more slowly than the flowering trees around them. Their needle leaves, stiff like those of most evergreens, are built to last, not for just a single summer but for years. A lifetime for alders, dogwoods, and other flowering trees of the Cascades may be 100 years; for the conifers it may be 500 years or more.

Douglas fir cones.

Flowering plants — whether they are wildflowers, grasses, or fragrant maple or cottonwood trees — all produce seed when sperm from pollen fertilizes an egg within the sheltered ovary of a flower. In the more primitive cone bearers, masses of pollen are produced on male cones — the red, yellow, or green budlike swellings on twigs in spring. The wind carries the profusion of tiny grains (there may be thousands of grains in a square inch of air when pollen is being shed) to the still-small female cone. It bears eggs "naked" on sheltering cone scales; they are not enclosed in an ovary as in flowering plants. The woody cone protects the growing seed, which is rich in oily stored food that nourishes the sprout until it grows roots and leaves to feed itself.

These oily seeds are an important food source for animals adapted to open the tough cones. The trees in turn "use" the animals to help reproduce the forest. Not only Clark's nutcrackers, but also Douglas and red squirrels, chipmunks, and mice hide or bury stores of cones or conifer seeds. Often these "planted" seeds, never dug up and eaten by the animal, are an important source of the forest's new seedlings.

Man has carried the relationship a step farther. In the intermittent years when the trees bear heavy seed crops, professional seed gatherers rob the caches where Douglas squirrels habitually bury dozens of cones in the mud. Foresters then use the squirrels' winter stores to plant new commercial timber.

The Wet Western Slope

Getting to know the typical plants of the Cascade forests takes time. But it is well worth it for the stories you will be able to read in the woods around you when you visit the mountains.

In the dense forests of the wet western slopes, Sitka spruce, with its bark of small neat scales and its messy cones, is a sign of low altitude. As the elevation increases Pacific silver fir and noble fir, symmetrical spire-shaped trees with upright cones, become more common and eventually predominate.

Today, droopy-topped, delicate-leaved western hemlock is the "climax" species of much of the western Cascades. This is because it grows well in the shade of other trees, and thus can mature under them and replace them when they die.

Douglas fir is also very common. It grows well in full sun; thus it has flourished naturally or been planted in vast burned or clearcut areas during this century of white man's rule in the mountains. In the driest areas of the west side, Douglas firs are likely to dominate, perhaps with a scattering of pine. Beneath these trees, you may find tough-leaved salal, or beargrass with wands of white flowers.

Sunny spots in the wet western Cascades are often waist- or shoulder-high with bracken fern or thimbleberry. Or they may be a tangle of vine maple, the only spot of bright fall color among the dark evergreens.

Steep slopes covered with shrubby Sitka alder are signs of heavy snow and avalanches. Like other shrubs of the steep slopes — white rhododendron and copper-flowered false azalea — Sitka alder has flexible but strong limbs that can bend under the impact and weight of heavy snow and still survive.

In wet, swampy areas, alder and cedar predominate, the latter with its stringy bark and fans of pungent, scaled twigs. Here delicate lady fern flourishes. Skunk cabbage and devil's club spread huge leaves to catch as much as possible of the light filtering through the dense canopy. Big leaves can flourish here because the plants do not need to be protected against water loss.

An area of more moderate moisture is indicated by tough-leaved deer fern, Oregon grape, and a group of flowers including white-flowered vanilla leaf, twisted-stalk, trillium, and false Solomon's seal. Trillium, star flower, and vanilla leaf spread their leaves flat — all from a single stem — to catch as much light as possible. False Solomon's seal and some ferns catch light in another way: their separate leaf segments are spread flat and do not shade one another.

Most deep shade flowers seem to be white or pale, making them highly visible to the pollinating insects of the forest. Some flowers have special adaptations that encourage ants to help them reproduce and spread: both

Vanilla leaf.

bleedingheart, with its drooping blossoms, and *Vancouveria,* a shy little white flower of deep shade, have a spongy white protrusion on their seeds. This seems to attract ants, which carry the seed away, eat the attachment, and leave the seed in a new spot where they plant may sprout.

On the Cascades' cool, wet western slopes, rain and melting snow wash away soluble salts, leaving the soil acid. Fungi and decaying conifer needles also release substances that help keep the soil acid. Thus acid-loving plants, such as huckleberry and salal, proliferate. There is also a thick layer of humus on this forest floor because evergreen needles decay much more slowly than the delicate leaves of deciduous trees, and the process is lengthened even further by the cool climate. In deepest shade, wet or dry, very few green plants grow; there is insufficient sunlight for them to manufacture food. The forest floor is bare except for rotting tree litter, oddly colored mushrooms, and parasites like ghostly Indian pipe.

Mushrooms are principal inhabitants of these old growth forests. A few days after the first rains of Indian summer, the Cascade forests bloom with these fungi. Mushrooms spring from rotten logs, root-rimmed hollows, and living trees. Purple, orange, gold, white, brown, blue, red, they are decorated with slime, scales, and veils. Some curl into flamelike fingers; others droop iciclelike teeth. Mushrooms cower under dead leaves, build shelves on stumps, spread elegant umbrellas a foot aboveground. Their smells are earthy and pugent, laced with licorice, violet, even garlic. As there are foul-smelling flowers, there are foul-smelling mushrooms that reek of rotting shrimp or tar.

Skunk cabbage.

Indian pipe.

Sulphur shelf mushrooms.

These bright-colored, odd-shaped bodies are both flowers and fruits, in a sense. They are the spore-bearing reproductive parts of fungi — plants that spend most of their lives as threads finer than a spider web, hidden underground or inside trees. Fungi do not make their own food as green plants do; they draw it from other organic matter, living or dead. A few types of fungi are pests. The edible honey mushroom, for example, kills trees. Most, however, aid other plants. In fact, without the hidden masses of fungal threads, the Cascades' thin and often poor soils might not support their giant evergreen forests. Earthworms and other soil animals that digest decaying vegetable matter do not flourish in these acid soils, among litter of tough, woody conifer needles. A major part of the job of soil-making is thus left to fungi that "eat" dead wood and leaves, turning them into forest soil that feeds other plants.

Some Cascade mushrooms are poisonous. More are edible. The great majority are simply useless to man as food — although squirrels, bears, and other animals may relish them. For some reason, many people seem to regard mushrooms as enemies. They kick or trample them along trails. This is a bit like deliberately picking wildflowers and dropping them to wilt. What is a toadstool to one person may be a delicacy to the forest animal or the mushroom hunter who is next along the trail.

A Miniature World of the Western Slope

In the damp, shady woods of the Western slope, mosses, liverworts, ferns, and their relatives create their own miniature forests under and on the big trees. Eons ago, tree-sized versions of club mosses and jungles of ferns flourished, and these nonflowering plants ruled the plant kingdom. Now shady forests are their retreat in a world dominated by flowering plants.

These "primitive" plants evolved before either cone bearing or flowering plants. As early venturers onto land, they show their ties to water by depending on moving water to help the male sperm swim to the female egg and begin a new plant's life. The rain and damp of wet forests aid these plants in much the same way that pollen-carrying insects help a wildflower meadow.

Moss grows on a rotting log.

Oak fern.

In the miniature forests created under the trees' protection, these "primitive" plants can be as particular about their habitats as if a few square feet were the whole world. In an area four feet square, you may find five kinds of mosses, each with its particular home. One hangs from a rock with thready stems and tiny "leaves," like a pale green beard. On the boulder's flat top a fernlike moss with fronds up to four inches long is found, branching and rebranching as it climbs. A rotting alder stick lying across the rock may be covered with a moss that resembles soft juniper or cedar twigs, its branches covered with tiny scales. Another moss with rosettes of round, dark green leaves, holding up red fruiting capsules, may grow on top of a crumbling cedar stump. The stump's vertical face is partly covered by yet another fernlike moss, this one with fronds that do not branch.

(Incidentally, on south-facing slopes, the north sides of boulders and stumps are often bare of moss. Trying to find your way by the old saying that "moss grows only on the north side of trees" is likely to lead you in circles in the Cascades.)

Other primitives are just as particular about habitat as the mosses. Some ferns prefer crevices in limestone; others are found almost exclusiverly near granite or similar "acid" rock. Although licorice fern — with its anise-flavored rhizomes that can be chewed to soothe sore throats — grows in company with common sword fern and lady fern, its hanging fronds usually droop from mossy rock faces or from maple trunks and limbs. This fern may stick to this environment because other ferns outcompete it on the forest floor, or because it has a high demand for calcium, supplied by the rocks and bark.

Deer fern.

Life from Death

In the forests of both eastern and western slopes, you may see seedlings flourishing in a straight row twenty feet long or more. These are the wards of a "nurse log" — a fallen ancestor that perhaps held the seedlings above the melting snow, or perhaps rotted into soil a little richer and better drained than the forest floor around it. The lively colony on this dead tree is nothing unusual. "Nurse logs" are not the only way by which dead trees add to the life of a forest. Dead or dying snags in a forest take on new life as homes, perches, or food sources for animals. The bleached skeleton, stretching a few clawlike limbs from a hollow trunk, may be more vital to forest life than a dozen of the green young trees around it. Bats and small birds roost under loose plates of bark that shelter them from wind and rain. The tops of high snags are favorite perches for birds like sparrow hawks and some flycatchers, which wait until an unsuspecting insect flies by, then sally out to snatch it.

Dead and dying trees no longer resist insect attacks, and the insects they harbor may attack and kill living trees. However, the borers and wood chewers that turn wood into a honeycomb of holes are food for woodpeckers that, braced and balanced by their stubby tails and back-turned toes, hammer out holes as large as themselves. The woodpeckers also build nest holes that may be used later by more than a dozen kinds of animals. Owls, sparrow hawks, squirrels, and some kinds of ducks, are among the animals that nest in old woodpecker holes or suitable natural hollows. Honeybees also use the hollow trees. You can watch the workers dancing at the entrance holes, signaling the location of flowers that will supply honey and pollen for the irregular combs in the hollow.

A forest without dead and hollow trees will be a forest poor in many of its "proper" birds and beasts. Understandably, a walk through a man-sowed, neatly-thinned plantation of commercial timber can seem monotonous and silent. Without death, the forest is robbed of much of its life.

Nurse log supporting a young hemlock along the Mount Si trail.

A raccoon caught during its nocturnal wanderings.

Forest Mammals

Animal watching becomes more difficult as you move from open alpine country to the forests lower on the Cascades. In fact, you could walk all a midsummer's day through evergreen forest and not see a single mammal.

Many woods animals are quiet and shy by comparison with the whistling, scolding pikas, marmots, and chipmunks of high meadows. Mountain beavers, hares, and porcupines, for example, do not broadcast possession of territory or warn of a stranger's approach in voices we hear. Even the Townsend chipmunk of lower forests is a shy creature compared with his relative, the yellow pine chipmunk of higher subalpine country. When the Townsend chipmunk scolds you, he usually stays hidden in the brush. Unless you recognize his "whisks," you could mistake them for a birdcall.

Forest wildlife is also difficult to see because many of these animals become active only at dusk or in darkness. Raccoons, mountain beavers, most mice, flying squirrels, snowshoe hares, skunks, porcupines, beavers, bobcats, cougars, and, of course, bats are among the animals that do much of their feeding between sunset and sunrise. Some, like raccoons and flying squirrels, are truly nocturnal. Others, like snowshoe hares, are most active at twilight. At midday, when we are most likely to be afoot, the animals are likely to be resting. (If you want to see the forest's night life, wait for a full moon or use a flashlight with a red bulb or clear red cover. Nocturnal animals do not seem to see the red rays.)

A fawn finds a safe resting spot in tall grass.

Animals are fewer in large stretches of unbroken evergreen forest. Old conifer trees that have never been logged and the younger stands of the same species and age planted by timber companies can seem lifeless and silent for the same reason: both lack the diversity of habitat needed for a varied animal population. Some animals have adapted to life in the deep evergreen forests, however. The little Douglas squirrel cuts cones and defends an aerial territory 100 feet in the air, using his long, bushy tail as balance, prop, and rudder when he moves from tree to tree. The marten, a bushy-tailed member of the weasel family, hunts the squirrels along the same branches. In order to have many animal species, however, there must be many kinds of food and many types of places in which to live and hide. The deepest evergreen forests, where conifers shade out most brush and flowers, seldom have this kind of variety.

In general, animals will be most varied on the edges of different kinds of habitats: places where forest meets meadow, where swamp touches brush and trees. Here you can expect to find the creatures of both kinds of habitats and some that use both (as mink hunt on land and in water, and deer browse in clearings and brushy spots but take shelter in woods).

Although it is hard to say anything nice about the scarred treeless patches left by clearcut logging, moderate logging in the dense western Cascade forests probably increased populations of several kinds of animals, from deer and snowshoe hares to skunks and beavers. The cleared areas left by loggers are apt to have plenty of the bulbs, berries, and insects the skunk seeks on his leisurely evening rambles. The grass, weeds, brush, and early succession deciduous forest that spring up in these sunny spots provide food for the grazers and browsers.

Yet, quiet as a Cascade forest may seem, a day's walk is likely to take you near more than a dozen kinds of mammals: moles, shrews, mice, voles, pack rats, snowshoe hares, squirrels, chipmunks, mountain beavers, porcupines, raccoons, deer, weasels, martens, fishers, coyotes, foxes, bobcats, bears, cougars, perhaps elk.

To learn to "see" the forest's shy wildlife you should go at the right seasons and the right times of day, listen as well as look, and watch not just for animals but for signs like tracks, droppings, paths, and burrows.

You may never see a mountain beaver. This dark brown, almost tailless rodent, about fourteen inches long, does much of its feeding at night, and often pulls plants — roots and all — down into its tunnel rather than come out and eat them. But you may see the mountain beaver's burrow entrances, about six inches in diameter and usually partly hidden by logs or the tangles of bracken and thimbleberry in the moist semiclearings it loves. Nearby you may spot little haystacks of greens it is drying for winter food.

These solitary and usually silent burrowers are worth looking for. Mountain beavers are found only in the Pacific Northwest. A living fossil, their bone and muscle structure is like that of primitive rodents, and they are the only members of a family that evolved long before families of modern rodents, such as squirrels and mice.

The snowshoe hare is another seldom-seen animal of brushy areas in Cascade forests. This is one of the best camouflaged animals in the woods, gray brown most of the year, but white in winter. (A subspecies in the nearly snow-free lowlands near Puget Sound stays brown year-round.) Well camouflaged and capable of fleeing rapidly, the snowshoe hare does not even dig burrows. It feeds at twilight and dawn, passing the day quietly under bushes in shallow depressions called "forms."

Near Lake Wenatchee, a tree-climbing bear finds a tenuous perch.

Snowshoe hares are highway builders. You can see the trails they make through their brushy home ranges. They and other animals use these paths for feeding and escape. The trails are easiest to spot in snow, when you can also recognize the up-to-six-inch tracks made by the broad, furry feet that give the snowshoe hare both its name, and its agility on loose snow. In winter, too, you can see signs of the hare's nibblings at twigs and bark. In summer, it is more likely to eat grass and softer greens.

Many animals gnaw at bark and the sugar-carrying sapwood beneath. Bears, porcupines, squirrels, elk, deer, beavers, and mountain beavers are among them. Often you can tell which animal made the raw yellow scar. For example, wood will usually show long vertical grooves where black bears have been gnawing. Bears seem to prefer smooth-barked conifers for gnawing, seeking their sugary sapwood especially in spring, probably because there are few other foods available. Although bears are technically carnivores, the black bears of the Cascades eat mostly berries, leaves, grass, and mushrooms. Oddly enough, prickly devil's club and peppery, foul-smelling skunk cabbage are two of their favorites.) Bark gnawing can injure or kill trees, of course. This has sometimes led to war between animals and timber growers, with the timber growers trying everything from guns and traps to repellents and imported predators.

You can tell when a red or Douglas squirrel lives nearby from the heaps of corncoblike cone stems and loose cone scales at the base of a tree. These squirrels are fond of eating from a particular perch, dropping the scales as they eat the seeds, and discarding the stripped stem.

Thorn-covered stalks of the devil's club.

Evidence of the beaver at work.

Season and sound are important for spotting these small, dark brown tree squirrels and their relatives, the rusty-sided Townsend chipmunks of Cascade forests. During their fall harvest season, you will see dozens where you saw none before. The squirrels trill challenges at one another and send cones clattering down from the treetops. They will scramble down a trunk to scold you with their "peooo, peooo, peooo." Chipmunks scamper across the trail or "whisk" at you from the bushes until you go away.

Like their high-altitude relatives, yellow pine chipmunks and golden-mantled ground squirrels, the forest squirrels and chipmunks can coexist because their differing habits cut competition. Although they like many of the same foods, red and Douglas squirrels climb high for cones and defend treetop territories, while Townsend chipmunks usually stick to bushes or the ground. Townsend chipmunks' tails, much thinner than those of tree squirrels, would not be as useful a balance or rudder on bending twigs or when leaping through the air.

At night, the flying squirrel spreads itself into a silky magic carpet and glides to gather many of the foods the Townsend chipmunk and Douglas and red squirrels seek. But here, too, differing habits reduce the rivalry: the flying squirrel is less a seed eater, and more a hunter of lichens, fungi, insects, and bird eggs. One of its main winter foods is the black thready lichen, *Alectoria,* that hangs from trees, once gathered by Indians for food. The flying squirrel does not store food for winter as do the Townsend chipmunk and red and Douglas squirrels.

Deer and elk, of course, are adept at vanishing during hunting season on both sides of the lower Cascades. They are most readily seen in late winter, when trees are bare and they descend to lower elevations to escape the worst snow and cold. Elk of the Mount Saint Helens area are likely to browse along roads, such as the one to Spirit Lake, during this season. (An easy way to see elk on the east side of the Cascades is to visit the headquarters of the Oak Creek Wildlife Recreation Area near Yakima. There, herds of elk are fed hay to keep them from invading neighboring farms and orchards that were their natural lowland wintering grounds.)

Elk probably are most interesting during their fall rut — when they should be watched from a respectful distance, as a bull elk in rut is extremely dangerous. At this time, the bull elk shrieks his "bugle" challenge — beginning incongruously as a falsetto and ending in a grunt. The fights between males, with hooves and antlers charging, are brutal and occasionally fatal.

If you are not sure whether you are watching deer or elk, elk are identified by heavier builds, stouter and more spreading antlers, manes of longer hair on chests and necks of males, and, if all else fails, by their rump patches, which are orange yellow, not white like those of deer.

Elk herd at the Oak Creek Wildlife Recreation Area near Yakima.

No matter how expert an animal watcher you become, you will never see some of the Cascades' native animal communities, because they no longer exist. The native Roosevelt elk was once much more widespread in the western Cascades. Today there are no elk on the Tolt River east of Seattle although the river took its name long ago from an Indian word meaning elk. Animals of humid evergreen forests, Roosevelt elk once ranged down as far as Puget Sound. They munched conifer tips, salal, maple, willow, alder, blackberry, huckleberry, devil's club and other tough forest fare as well as grass, wildflowers, and ferns. Deer fern was a favorite with them then, as it is now with deer.

Today, the only elk in the Cascades that come close to being pure native stock are those in the Mount Saint Helens area. Others are mostly transplanted Rocky Mountain elk — stockier, paler, with wider-spreading antlers. (Larger numbers of Roosevelt elk do survive in the Olympic Mountains, however.)

The gray wolf and the grizzly bear, carnivores large enough to threaten cattle, were hunted mercilessly in the Cascades, as almost everywhere in the nation. A few grizzlies probably survive in the North Cascades, but wolves seem to have vanished from the range.

Porcupine.

Cougars, the big six-foot cats also called pumas or mountain lions, survive in the mountains today. Although they once ranged down to Puget Sound, hunting by man and cougars' natural shyness made them retreat to the mountain forests. Here, they are not in danger of extinction; in fact, they seem to be making a comeback now that they are no longer hunted for bounties, but only for sport.

Fishers probably were never common. Today, they are strictly protected as a rare species. Earlier fur trapping cut their numbers, and so did the destruction of much of the dense evergreen forest that is their natural home. These dark brown members of the weasel family, up to forty inches long, can hunt easily on the ground or in trees, like their smaller relatives, the martens. (The marten is only about two feet long, and has an orange throat patch that the fisher lacks.) Fishers are among the few animals that regularly kill porcupine. Apparently fishers attack the porky head-on, clawing and biting at its face until it weakens. The fisher then flips it over to begin feeding either at the belly or at the head. This habit has made fishers one of the few predators protected and encouraged because of man's economic interests. In regions where fishers had disappeared, they have been reintroduced to control the porcupines that gnaw and kill timber trees.

There are animals of the far north whose habitat runs south along the cold spines of mountain ranges: wolverines with fur that sheds moisture and frost (and is therefore sought by trappers for the ruffs of parka hoods); lynxes with big, furry feet that permit movement over loose snow in pursuit of their main winter food, the similarly-equipped snowshoe hare. Probably neither lynx nor wolverine was ever common in the Cascades. Both are most likely to be found in the North Cascades. The wolverine, a versatile member of the weasel family that looks more like a small bear and can climb, swim, dig, or run, is strictly protected as a rare species in Washington. The ghostly, yellow gray lynx, with long hind legs supporting a high, bobtailed rump, is still trapped as a furbearer.

Despite instances like those mentioned, man-caused changes have not obscured the outlines of native animal communities in the Cascades, as they have elsewhere. You can still see the relationships of animals to their natural habitats and to one another in the Cascades. On the western slopes of the range, for example, mammals from snowshoe hares to cougar and bobcat tend to have darker, rustier coats than on the more open eastern slopes — a difference that probably makes for better camouflage.

Cascade animals also adapt to the different mountain seasons by making radical changes in their diets. Porcupines, for example, may eat mostly greens in summer but switch to the inner bark of trees in winter. Still another seasonal adaptation is migration between mountaintops and lowland valleys. Although animals as small and slow moving as porcupines may migrate, you are most likely to see this in deer. Shortly before the first winter storms, hundreds of deer may move down to lowland wintering grounds, perhaps forewarned by changes in barometric pressure, which they can sense.

The waddling porcupine and the shuffling skunk are two Cascade animals you are likely to see because they move slowly and rather boldly. They have little need to move quickly because of their built-in defenses: sharp quills in the porcupine; reeking, eye-burning scent in the skunk. It may even be an advantage for them to move slowly and be recognized as the threats they are. When threatened they tend to "stand and be recognized" rather than flee. The porcupine raises its quills and waves its tail; the skunk stamps its feet and also waves a plumy tail.

An evening grosbeak perches on a campfire grill. Like crossbills, these birds feed on ashes.

Forest Birds

Like mammal watching, bird watching is more difficult in deep woods than in open country. In tall evergreen forests, most of the birds you see may be flocks moving quickly through the treetops over 100 feet above your head. These fast-moving flocks, calling as they go, are likely to be among the Cascades' most typical and interesting birds. They may, for example, be red crossbills (or rarely, white-winged crossbills), birds that have evolved physical features and habits that adapt them to life in cone-bearing forests. The upper and lower mandibles of their beaks cross like two hooks, which they use to pry apart tightly shut cone scales. From these they extract seeds with their unusually long tongues.

Crossbills do not always stay in the treetops. You may catch a closer look at the brick red males and yellowish olive females when they fly down to pick through the ashes of old campfires. Apparently they eat the ashes for mineral salts, in the same way mammals eat mineral clay or salt at salt licks.

There are other types of treetop flocks. Pine siskins — small, brown, striped birds, their wings touched with yellow — are common, interrupting their chirping, tinkling calls with buzzy "shrees." Their stout, short, conical bills, adapted for seed cracking, show that they are members of the finch family, like the crossbills. A similar bill is found on a big bird of conifer tops, the evening grosbeak, also a member of the finch family. Handsome males of this species look as if dressed for a formal evening in black, white, and gold.

As is the case with mammals, relatively few birds are adapted to live in the deep, monotonous evergreen forests. You are likely to see more variety in broken woods or at the edges of forests and clearings. Wherever seen, forest birds are well worth the patience it takes to get to know them.

Bald eagle surveys the Skagit River near Marblemount.

On the mossy forest floor, you might see the little chickenlike spruce grouse nicknamed "fool hen" for its tameness. This grouse looks like a bit of rotting wood, thanks to its mottled black plumage. Its brown-spotted eggs, laid in a ground nest, are just as invisible. The males are obvious in spring, however, when they "drum" — fluttering from branch to ground and back with a rattling of their wings.

The winter wren half hisses its combative song from the deep forest, where it forages along mossy logs and trunks, nervous and scolding as any wren.

The varied thrush's coloring — rather like a robin's, but with a black band across the chest and orange stripes on eyes and wings — is surprisingly good camouflage in the forest of reddish trunks. The thrush family, which includes the familiar robin, shows how members of big bird families cut down competition by having special "preferences" about where they live. You are likely to hear the hermit thrush's long, clear note followed by a trill in open and subalpine forests. The veery's descending couplets are most likely to come from the moist bottoms of brush and deciduous woods. The varied thrush quavers a beautiful, single note from deep evergreen shade. But you will see all three hopping along the ground for food, like the familiar backyard robin.

Gray or Canada jay.

Some forest birds have the kinds of names that cause people to make fun of bird watchers: creeper, kinglet, nuthatch. Yet the names are there for precise reasons; they describe the distinctions that make bird watching so fascinating. The creeper moves slowly up trunks, looking like a bit of brown bark, finding hidden mites with its long, curved bill. You will probably not see one unless you hear its exquisitely delicate song, like the notes of a distant, old-fashioned music box. The kinglet is a tiny, quick-moving, gray bird usually seen fluttering from twig to twig. However, when it comes to courtship or disputes with rival males, the kinglet is transformed: he fans his tail, raises a dazzling crown of red and yellow feathers on his head, and flutters bravely at his rival. With a big head and short body and tail, the nuthatch can hardly be called pretty. Nor is it musical, with a nasal "nyat" call that may be repeated over 100 times in quick succession. However, it does have the unique habit of walking upside-down on limb bottoms or hanging head-downwards on trunks. It also digs out its own nest hole like the woodpecker and carefully smears pitch on the entrance.

In bushy forests you may see a small hawk dash through the undergrowth after a kinglet or other small bird. The hunter is likely to be a sharp-shinned hawk, brown-streaked if a juvenile, or gray with reddish breast if an adult. Hawks' shapes provide clues to their hunting styles. Short-winged, long-tailed hawks — like the sharp-shinned hawk and the Cooper's hawk — hunt with short bolts and sudden turns through brush and treetops. The same quick-steering shape (the tail probably helps the bird brake as well as steer) is found in other brush birds, like towhees and lowland bushtits.

Steller's jay.

In cleared areas fast-flying birds, such as bird-hunting falcons and fly-catching sparrow hawks, overtake their prey on the wing. They have long, pointed, fast-beating wings and medium-length tails with squarish ends. Birds that soar in search of unwary prey — like the red-tailed hawks and golden eagles seen circling on mountain updrafts — have long, broad wings and short, broad, fan-shaped tails.

Even this short sketch cannot end without mentioning the camp robber or gray jay, the familiar gray ghost that floats down to share your camp meal whether you will or not. Even its whistle has a ghostly sound. Like the dark blue, black-hooded Steller's jay that often replace it in lower altitude forests, the camp robber is an all-purpose bird. It will happily eat insects, seeds, or meat, sometimes stealing bird eggs and bird young. It feeds either on the ground or in the treetops with an all-purpose bill — one broad enough to swallow large chunks of food, long enough to probe, and strong enough to hammer. Its hammering could be mistaken for a woodpecker's. When flying away with a morsel, it may dine in some safer spot or cache its catch for the future. The camp robber has even adapted to human whim. What other bird around your forest camp is likely to take a handout literally from your hand?

Mistletoe – the deadly forest parasite.

The Dry Eastern Slope

Though western slope forests are shaped by shade, damp, and snow, the eastern slopes are generally formed by two quite different forces: drought and fire.

Forests here look different. Trees common on the western slopes — shade-loving western yew and western hemlock, for example — are found only in the damper areas of the eastern slopes. Most common, as you descend from a subalpine forest, are stands of grand fir and Douglas fir. Lower down, the forest changes to mostly Douglas fir and red-trunked ponderosa pine.

A strange and deadly forest guest inhabiting the Cascades is the mistletoe, a chartreuse decoration on the red-trunked pines. In late summer its seeds are shot through the air at speeds of up to ninety feet per second. Once the sticky seed has found a branch, a long period of secret work begins. For more than two years the mistletoe puts its energy into producing tiny flowers that harbor nectar and exude scents to attract pollinating insects, and into ripening its pressurized fruit. As it blooms and grows, the deadly guest drives its host tree into a suicidal frenzy. The juicy little plant sucks water, minerals, and nutrients from the limb into which it has sunk its roots. The tree pumps more and more nutrients into the invaded limb, which grows faster and faster while others die. Eventually, however, the tree lacks a sufficient supply of green leaves to nourish its bulk and it dies — after, in effect, keeping the mistletoe alive as long as possible.

Rolling hills near Winthrop with Mount Gardner in the distance.

Trees line a sheltered ravine near Rattlesnake Creek.

Trees are more scattered here than on the western slopes; the east-slope forest is dappled with sunlight, rather than dim from the shade of close-set evergreens. Big-leaved, light-catching ground covers give way to a group of shrubs with small, light-colored leaves that reflect sunlight and save water: snowberry, wild rose, serviceberry (Juneberry). Gardeners will recognize some common plants here, like wild rose, that prefer the neutral soil. (On this drier eastern side, the soil tends to be neutral rather than acid. Because of the lack of rain and snowmelt, the soil retains its salts. Forests fires also return humus to the soil as ashes, making the soil more basic.)

Dry slopes are spotted with tough-leaved and twisted evergreen shrubs: snowbush, pinemat manzanita, and kinnikinnick. These are northern fragments of the chaparral — similar stands of drought-tolerant evergreens with tough leaves and twisted limbs, covering miles of dry mountains in Oregon and California.

On creek fringes in the eastern Cascades, quaking aspen and cottonwood with fragrant leaf buds supplant the alder and fragrant-blossomed bigleaf maple that border many western-slope streams. Aspen and cottonwood are close relatives. Both have pale, shiny leaves that reflect light and heat. Both have silky-haired seeds that the wind can waft long distances — perhaps to the next stream bed. Both spread by means of suckers — underground roots that link the trees in a grove and even allow them to send water and nutrients back and forth.

Meadows are common on the eastern slope mountains. Forest clearings have formed for a variety of reasons: the ground may be too dry or too wet for trees; snowslides may brush away trees on avalanche slopes; fires, logging, or windthrows may have cleared the land; a lake may have silted up; or a beaver pond may have been abandoned and drained. Magenta-flowered fireweed, its leaves crimson in autumn, loudly signals an area recently logged or burned. The tassels on its seeds, lending the plant a cottony look in late summer, help the wind carry fireweed seed to bare spots before other plants with slower modes of transportation arrive. In later years, other flowers and shrubs outcompete the fireweed, which moves on to new sites. Damp spots in clearings are filled with juicy, knee-high greens that crunch underfoot, such as fuzzy-flowered waterleaf. Drier places — like the bald hilltops where wind blows winter snow away and rain drains off quickly — are often grassy, with wildflowers like yellow balsamroot, blue lupine and larkspur, white yarrow, red paintbrush.

Meadows like these are almost everywhere in the eastern Cascades, often only short hikes away from the road. For example, explore the country around Redtop Lookout near the Blewett Pass Highway/U.S. 97, or the higher parts of the L.T. Murray Wildlife Recreation Area and the area around Tamarack Springs south of the Snoqualmie Pass Highway/ Interstate 90.

Not surprisingly, fire is more common on the dry eastern slopes of the Cascades than on the wet western side. For centuries, Indians increased the frequency of fires, burning clearings to keep wild foods from being shaded out, and setting fire to underbrush for easier hunting. Before the white man clamped his controls on forest fires early in this century, the eastern slopes of the Cascades might have seen fire more often than once every twenty years. However, these were not wildfires moving 100 miles an hour, destroying everything in their paths. They were usually low ground fires, moving slowly, giving animals time to flee or to take to their burrows. Such fires eat up forest litter and convert it to soluble nutrients, leaving the big trees standing and still alive.

Many plants of the eastern Cascades have adapted to fires and have developed special survival methods. Three of the most common east side conifers — western larch, ponderosa pine, and Douglas fir — have bark so thick that older trees are almost fireproof. Lodgepole pine and snowbush have a phoenixlike way of surviving. Though they are thin-barked and easily killed by fire, their seeds stay alive for years, germinating only when the heat of another fire opens the snowbush seeds or the lodgepole cones. Aspen and cottonwood can sprout again from underground suckers if fire burns the tree above.

This same survival mechanism of springing back from the roots is used by those remarkable plants that appear on the eastern slopes almost wherever trees disappear — grasses. Even some mushrooms seem to have a special affinity for burned-over areas. The delicious morel, looking like a scorched cone itself with its ridged and pitted brown cap, often sprouts in abundance in the spring after a summer forest fire.

Burn near Golden Lakes, Mount Rainier National Park.

Dry Country of the Eastern Cascades

At the dry easternmost edge of the Cascades, forests of red and black-trunked pines thin out. Between brushy fringes in canyons, shiny with cottonwood and aspen, the rocky foothills are left to sagebrush and bunch grass.

Spring is the time to visit this near desert. State-owned game ranges that stretch along the east-running ridges are safe and silent without the whiz of hunters' bullets. While the high country is still snowbound, lava canyons and open, rolling ridges in these foothills can give a mountain lover both a sense of isolation and a great sweep of space. (The Oak Creek Wildlife Recreation Area near Yakima; the L.T. Murray near Ellensburg; and the Colockum in the hills between Ellensburg and Wenatchee all run from forest to near desert and offer you miles of dirt roads and short trails to explore.)

Spring is also the easiest time to see the life of the dry country. Hills that will later be parched gray or brown are splashed with color, as flowers rush to bloom and set seed before the moisture is gone. Animals that will later move to higher, lusher ground or disappear underground can be seen, along with their incautious young. With luck, you can watch baby ground squirrels wrestle outside their burrows, and fluffy coyote pups make their first awkward attempts at hunting. In spring you can see the colorful, noisy birds of open country perform their mating rites.

In this season, the dry country shows the richness that made it hospitable to hunting and gathering tribes. Camas, brodiaea, and wild onion wave blue-, white-, or rose-colored blossoms to mark their edible bulbs. Bitterroot flowers are flags above another Indian staple. Clumps of bright yellow sunflowerlike balsamroot promise oily seeds and pungent roots that can be baked. Miner's lettuce and other spring greens flourish in canyons. White serviceberry flowers promise a harvest later on.

Camas in the Wenatchee Mountains.

Balsamroot.

Prickly-pear cactus.

Drought Plants

Plants on the parched edge of the Cascades show many of the drought adaptations also found in high meadows. You will see low, clumpy varieties with pale leaves that are fleshy and fuzzy, or tough-skinned and leathery. Stonecrop and thorny prickly-pear cacti, with their incredibly delicate, tissuelike pink and yellow rosettes in spring, have fleshy, water-storing leaves. Wild buckwheat with fuzzy clumps of leaves stains the rock fields here with cerise and yellow flowers, just as it does on rocky summits above timber. A version of the woodsy violet lives in sagebrush country: although the little purple flower is the same as the one that nods shyly in the shade, the sagebrush violet's leaves have grown gray and leathery against the bright sun.

Bitterroot.

Foothill plants show other adaptations to dryness seldom found in alpine country. Annuals like salmon-and-sky-blue collomia and scarlet gilia send up spindly plants, which seem to put nearly all their energy into producing their bright trumpet flowers and seeds. This done, the plant dies, leaving the seed to survive drought and cold until the next spring.

At the extreme of this kind of life are the "ephemerals" — plants that have active, aboveground lives only in the short wet spring. Rosy and pale wild onions of the dry country and the Indian staple, bitterroot, are among these here-today, hidden-tomorrow plants. Leaves appear first and wither away. Then, still in springtime, flowers form. Seed is left to dry aboveground, and the plant spends the rest of the year as a buried root or bulb.

Pungent leaves are common in the dry country. Sage, balsamroot, rabbit brush, yarrow are just a few. The leaf fragrances that make walks in sagebrush country, or in sunny conifer woods, so delightful have a rather prosaic origin. Without plentiful rain to wash away by-products of food-making in the plant's leaves, dry-land plants often develop pungent oils that let the sun evaporate their wastes. Besides eliminating wastes, the strong-smelling and strong-flavored oils may defend the plant against insects and other grazers tempted to eat the leaves.

Kingdoms of Grass and Sage

The dry hills of the eastern Cascades are full of the unexpected and the varied. There are licorice-scented wild mints along streams, delicate *Woodsia* ferns among dry rocks. Red- and white-barked birches fringe streams in the north. To the south are scattered little kingdoms of oak trees, nourishing colonies of birds and squirrels with their acorns. A succession of white-flowered shrubs decorates the hills: serviceberry, then chokecherry, then snowbush, mock orange, clematis, elderberry.

The true rulers of the dry country, however, are grass and sagebrush. In some ways, they are locked together in a struggle for territory. Sagebrush is a typical dry-land shrub, deep-rooted, with twisting branches and relatively few small, fuzzy, grayish leaves rich in pungent oils. It shares a tolerance of alkaline or basic soils with several of its common companions, such as thin-leaved rabbit brush and darker green greasewood. In this dry country, the leaching that made soil acid in wet forests is reversed: there is not enough water to wash salts from the soil. On flats or sinks, you may even see whitish alkali deposits where salts have been brought to the surface with water that then evaporated. Sage and some of its companions thrive in this kind of soil, and the litter of leaves they drop seems to make the soil still more alkaline, presumably to help discourage competing plants.

Grasses are among the most remarkable plants on our planet. They seem to take over virtually wherever trees cannot thrive. The staff of life to grazing animals from grasshoppers to bison, grass has unusual survival abilities. Many grass leaves are unusually flexible, springing back when they are bent to the ground by hooves. Unlike ordinary leaves, they continue to grow from their bases when nipped off at the tops. To survive drought, many grasses can curl their leaves to reduce water loss. Many form turf, a thick mat of roots that helps prevent soil erosion and combats would-be invading plants. Some grasses also harbor microorganisms or secrete chemicals that deter trees from invading the prairie.

In the abstract, one can picture a "bunchgrass zone" in the Cascades, lying where conditions are between those of the wetter pine woods and the drier sagebrush zone stretching east across the Columbia Basin's flatlands. In the real foothills, however, sage and similar shrubs and grasses mix and mingle. Some forests fade directly into sagebrush; sage and grass may grow together; or you may find sage on the dry south side of a hill and grass on the moister north. Such combinations are natural. But the natural territories of grass and sage have also been much changed by man.

Early settlers often described the bunchgrass of the eastern Cascades as being "up to a horse's belly." However, overgrazing by livestock, starting in the late nineteenth century when the range was free to cattlemen and sheepmen, killed some of the tall grasses. In many places the native species seem to have been replaced permanently by shorter grasses or weedy flowers such as yarrow. In other areas, overgrazing allowed sagebrush to invade and conquer what once was grassland.

On the other hand, much of the sagebrush land that once was home to characteristic animals has been converted to grassland or farms by brush fires or cultivation. As a result, some dry-land animals, like the sage grouse, are much less common than they were.

Dry-Country Animals

Animals, like plants, adapt to the near desert of the Cascade's eastern foothills in varying ways. Long-legged mammals like the pronghorn antelope or the coyote, for example, can travel great distances for food or water. The pronghorn, fastest of North American mammals (and perhaps the only one that really relishes sagebrush), can bound to a spring three miles away and be back in twenty minutes.

Many dry-land animals save energy and water by resting in the heat of the day. Pronghorns are most active at dawn and dusk in summer. Jackrabbits rest in shallow depressions under bushes during the day, which is the reason you see them in the beam of your headlights more often than in sunlight.

Some animals are physically able to live with less water than others. There is moisture in greens, meat, even seeds, and all animals produce some water as they digest food with the help of stomach bacteria. Some desert animals make such good use of these sources of water that they can survive though they seldom or never drink. The rattlesnakes and lizards of the eastern Cascades need very little water to supplement their diets.

The sagebrush meadow mouse and the western harvest mouse are dry country dwellers found in the eastern foothills, where they scurry through small territories on tiny trails. The pale gray sagebrush meadow mouse, living mainly on greens, seems able to survive indefinitely without water. The western harvest mouse, which eats and stores seeds, can live on salt water — possibly an adaptation for survival in deserts where water may be brackish or alkaline.

Other animals survive heat and drought by spending most of their lives in cool underground tunnels. The pocket gopher, for example, spends almost its whole life alone in a burrow system it defends from other pocket gophers except at mating season. It eats roots or seeds and greens harvested outside and stored in its lair for winter. This rodent uses its long front teeth to tunnel through the earth, and its powerful claws to push the loosened dirt away. These subterranean animals range from high meadows to lowlands, mostly on the Cascades' eastern slopes. You will find their tunnelings in soil so rocky and barren that it is surprising the little rodents can dig and find enough to eat. Their burrows and those of other animals have an important effect on the soil: by loosening it and leaving excrement and buried food, they in effect plow and fertilize the land, making life easier for plants and other animals.

The ground squirrels and the little gray least chipmunk of dry country are like ephemeral wildflowers; they survive by spending only a bit of each year active and aboveground. These rodents can become dormant not only during winter's cold but also during summer's heat and drought. They may spend two-thirds of each year in hibernation or estivation (as the summer sleep is called).

The little, light gray least chipmunk, shy and well camouflaged, is seldom seen. Its burrow is inconspicuous — a small hole usually under a bush, log, or rock. The faintly spotted ground squirrel of the eastern foothills, on the other hand, has an easy-to-spot colonial burrow. These burrows often have several entrances, made obvious by earth grazed or trampled bare and mounds of dirt cast out of tunnels. Inside are escape routes, chambers for rearing young or for hibernation, even drains to keep the dens from filling with water.

Seeds of lupine and balsamroot are favorite ground squirrel foods. If you have not spied the squirrel hiding in a flower clump, it is startling to see flowers vanish as it pulls them down. Ground squirrels also climb low trees for food, particularly the big California squirrels with long, bushy tails similar to those of tree squirrels. These California ground squirrels, which crossed the Columbia and invaded southeastern Washington early in this century, often dig burrows on slopes, while the shorter-tailed Townsend ground squirrel is at home with a burrow on flat land. Not surprisingly, the invading California ground squirrels have moved into fairly woodsy, hilly country, leaving the dry brush and flatlands to the native Townsend ground squirrels.

The speedy pronghorn antelope is rarely seen in Washington.

Badger – denizen of the dry lands.

With so many burrowing animals, one would expect to find predators adapted to hunt and eat them — and there are. The coyote is a good digger. The real specialist, however, is the badger, another member of the versatile weasel family, which seems to provide a hunter for every situation. The badger is a grayish animal about thirty inches long, with a white and dark brown mask and a squat, flattened look, as if it had been run over. Not a fast runner, it uses its big, powerful, long-clawed feet to dig for ground squirrels and other rodents in their burrows. The badger also catches other animals and insects aboveground and will use its digging talents here, too: it may dig a small hole and lie in wait for unwary prey. The badger lives in underground burrows, often enlarged ground squirrel dens. A badger hole is usually easy to distinguish by its size — generally eight inches in diameter or more.

Dry-Country Birds

The hills of sage and bunchgrass, sprinkled with pines and cut by brush-fringed canyons, are a bird watcher's paradise in spring. Many birds are drawn to its varied habitats — from desert sage to moist stream bank. Their light, bright feathers are common and easy to spot in this sunny, open country.

Sitting still on a sage hill above an oak-edged creek, you can watch the bright blue lazuli bunting repeat its simple, cheerful song from a high bush. A pair of black-and-yellow orioles call as they forage together in the brush. A meadowlark, also marked black and yellow, sings its liquid songs from bushes and fence posts around its territory. Happily for us, this most beautiful of singers is a lusty polygamist who takes several mates and sings through most of the summer days. Near a wooded creek, a rufous-sided towhee with orange, white, and black feathers complains as it scrambles for insects under a bush. A western tanager flashes a bright yellow body and bright red head in the treetops. A flock of little yellow warblers flutter from branch to branch.

The spring singing season brings an added attraction in this open country. Perhaps because birds can see one another easily, many have special looping, fluttering flights or strutting displays as part of their mating rituals. These showy exhibitions seem to be less common among birds of thick forests, where sound alone is more often used to entice a female or drive away rival males.

In sage country, you again meet the tough little horned lark, which also nests on treeless mountaintops. In spring these birds move in pairs, pecking along the ground like small, dark chickens. The male horned lark has a courtship flight: he circles upward, singing, then dives. The sage thrasher, a robin-sized, gray brown bird of sagebrush country, has a zigzag spring flight accompanied by wing flutters as he lands. The nighthawk — not a hawk at all, but an insect-eating relative of the whippoorwill — adds to the spring displays his stunning dive ending in a "boom" caused by air rushing through his feathers.

Magpies, exotic looking with their long tails and striking black and white plumage, perform a kind of group display ritual: flocks gather and erect their head feathers, fan their tails, and hover. (Although these common birds, with their harsh cries, are often condemned as pests and predators because they eat other birds' eggs and young, they have their positive side. They eat carrion and help their fellow birds by building large, roofed nests, which others have been known to use after the magpies have abandoned them.)

Perhaps the showiest mating rituals of the eastern Cascades are those of grouse. During May and June, hoots of the blue grouse seem to come from every stream canyon, sounding like four or five beats of a tom-tom. The much larger sage and sharp-tailed grouse that once inhabited the open sagebrush country are growing rare as farmers clear brush cover and convert their traditional mating grounds into pastures and irrigated farms. But the birds still gather during the annual courtship season in spring on "booming grounds" at the dry edge of the foothills. Dozens of males assemble in the early morning on a few acres. They stage ritual "fights" and "dances" — beating their wings, fanning their striking tails, strutting, turning, and inflating and bouncing the big, light-colored air sacs on their throats. In this curious ceremony, the displays seem to impress only other males, discouraging them from invading a territory (which the same male may hold for several years running). Females, gathered demurely in clumps on the mating grounds, seem more attracted to particular places than to particular birds; they usually mate with whichever males hold the territories deemed the most "desirable" — to the grouse, anyway. (If you wish to see them, Washington State Game Department offices in Yakima and Wenatchee as well as Audubon societies lead excursions to the courtship areas in spring. Many of the grouse later migrate up to wetter subalpine meadows, where you might see them feeding along the ground.)

Eagle and magpie feeding on a kill near Entiat.

Takhlakh Lake and Mount Adams.

Man and the Cascades

The Cascades are rich in human events as well as in natural history. Though the Indians did not make their homes amid the high peaks, foothill tribes hunted, fished, and gathered edible roots and berries in the mountains. They crossed the passes to trade, and wove legends about the peaks, plants, and animals of the range. Settlers' struggles, swindles, and booms, as they set out to subdue the Cascades, shaped much of what we see today — including some modern problems concerning man's management of the mountains.

The Cascades in Indian Legend

Before the Changer came and made things more or less as they are, Indian legends of the Cascades say that animals and even mountains walked about and talked like people.

One mountain in the Olympic Range west of Puget Sound had two wives. The younger wife, still a growing girl, quarreled constantly with the older wife and with their husband. Finally the young wife took her son and a basket of food and moved across Puget Sound. As she crossed, she dropped a piece of salmon from her basket — and salmon have run in the Sound ever since. In her new home she grew to be the highest of the Cascade volcanoes, Mount Rainier. Her infant son is the bump on the east flank of the mountain, Little Tahoma Peak.

There are many such tales of the time when mountains were alive, and many versions of each tale. The loosely knit tribes along the edges of the Cascades did not hesitate to borrow from their neighbors, inserting references to local rocks, rivers, plants, and animals. The tales describe how people who needed and used the wilds may have regarded these mountains. Some have a moral "lesson"; others explain the origins of names or places. Still others are simply amusing — and very earthy — stories, told in camps at night to entertain elders and reward the young.

The Indians who lived southeast of the Cascades credited Mount Adams with stealing life-giving roots, seeds, bulbs, and berries from other mountains to the south. This thievery led to a great battle between Mount Adams and Mount Hood, the volcano whose near-perfect cone rises south of the Columbia River in Oregon. The two volcanoes hurled fiery rocks and flame at each other until Mount Hood struck off the head of Moung Adams and scattered it as great boulders on her slopes. Thus, Mount Adams has a blunt, flattened top.

In other legends, Mount Adams and Mount Hood were rivals who fought for the love of Mount Saint Helens, guardian of the Bridge of the Gods that spanned the Columbia River. The battle broke the bridge or, in some versions, the Great Spirit destroyed the bridge to punish the rivals for breaking the peace. There may have been such a bridge: a huge slide from the north wall of the Columbia Gorge may have blocked the river partially as recently as the eighteenth century.

Indians west of the Cascades often told of Changer who made things as they are today. For some tribes, Changer was Snoqualm, or Moon, commemorated in the Cascade's Snoqualmie Pass and Snoqualmie Falls. The legend of Snoqualm as Changer begins when two sisters went to dig bracken-fern roots on the prairie near Snoqualmie Falls. While spending the night under the stars, the younger sister made a wish that a winking white star would be her husband the red star her older sister's. When they awakened, the wish had come true. They found themselves in the sky country with their new husbands. One day, while digging for fern roots, the sisters accidentally broke through the bottom of the sky world and found themselves looking at their old home. Secretly, they braided a rope of cedar limbs and lowered themselves taking with them the older sister's infant, called Snoqualm or Changer. The sisters arrived at the upper Snoqualmie valley near the present town of North Bend, where today's busiest cross-state highway heads into the Cascades. The rope was left dangling from the sky, and for years people swung on it, kicking off from lone Mount Si north of the valley and swinging to Rattlesnake Mountain on the south.

Changer brought his salmon children with him to the world of man, and ordered them to run in the rivers and be food for the people. In his wanderings, he used great powers to change things into what they are today. One man sharpening a spear to kill Changer was changed into an antlered deer; another who was spearing fish was transformed into a great blue heron.

East of the Cascades, legends often assign a role similar to Changer's to Spelyai, or Coyote: crafty, libidinous, but generally friendly toward man. One of the many tales of Coyote begins at Cle Elum Lake, a glacier-made lake, now enlarged by a dam, east of Snoqualmie Pass. Whishpoosh, or Beaver, lived in the lake, and Coyote went to fight him. During the

Snoqualmie Falls.

struggle, the two thrashed out of the lake and down what is now the Yakima River. They gouged out the Yakima's canyon and crashed through the Cascade Mountains, forming the Columbia Gorge that divides Oregon and Washington. At last they reached the ocean, and Whishpoosh died. Coyote, half-drowned, climbed out onto the beach and cut up Beaver's corpse. He threw the parts around the West, and each part became a tribe with appropriate talents. If the tribe came from Beaver's leg, for instance, its members were excellent runners; if from his eye, they had keen sight.

In other legends, Coyote traveled upriver — usually the Columbia River, but sometimes the Cowlitz or others. At every place where the people let him sleep with one of their daughters, he built a whirlpool or a falls where Indians could easily spear salmon. Wherever people refused, he blocked the river with a big rock or dam, so that the salmon could not pass. This is why Chelan Falls, for example, restricts salmon from swimming up into Lake Chelan.

Coyote and Changer are not the only main characters in legends of the Cascade tribes. According to one tale, all the animals once banded together to steal fire from the sky country. Nuthatch, a small brown bird that hangs upside-down on limbs, fastened their ladder of arrows to the sky. Once in sky country, all of the animals hid — except Beaver, the least ticklish of the group; he stretched out in the sky people's fish trap. When the sky people found him, they clubbed him, laid him by their fire, and skinned him. While this ticklish procedure was carried out, Beaver was able to observe where they hid their fire at night. That night, all the animals attacked. Beaver seized some fire, reclaimed his skin, and they all fled back to earth. Only Rattlesnake and Gartersnake were left behind. When they finally tumbled back to earth, they landed on opposite sides of the mountains. This is why there are no rattlesnakes west of the Cascades.

Local landmarks familiar to the Indians were often the subjects of legends. Jagged Sawtooth Ridge, south of Mount Rainier, was said to be the result of a rock-throwing contest between two brothers, Enumclaw and Kapoonis. After breaking the ridge into sharp-pointed peaks, Enumclaw, who was very strong, was turned into thunder. Kapoonis, who had a fiery spirit acquired by bathing in mineral springs near the head of the Cowlitz River, became lightning.

Some Cascade Mountain lakes and peaks were believed to be the homes of powers that could be dangerous to trespassers. The lashing tail of a monster was said to cause the sudden waves that endangered canoes on Lake Chelan. Spirit Lake, reflecting Mount Saint Helens, was named for the Indian legends attached to it; some bands shunned it as a home for the vengeful spirits of outcast Indians. In another tale, two brothers were changed into water creatures when they disregarded warnings and ate salmon caught near the lake.

Mount Si seen from Rattlesnake Ridge.

Another story of preternatural powers in the wilds was written down by Theodore Winthrop, an adventurous young New Englander who crossed the range in 1853 with only an Indian guide for company. This tale of the miser of Mount Rainier may be the Cascades' best-known legend.

The legend tells of a man who lived near the base of the great volcano. Although he was a good hunter and fisherman, he thought of nothing except acquiring more strings of shell money, or hiaqua. He did not attend feasts where he would have to exchange gifts. In hard times he sold tough meat at high prices to his neighbors. To teach him a lesson, Elk, his guardian spirit, told him he could find all the shell money he wanted at the summit of Mount Rainier.

The miser started up the volcano in the darkness of early morning. At sunrise, he reached the summit and found the black lake in a crater that the elk had described. At the far edge of the lake were three stones: one shaped like a salmon head, one like a camas bulb, the third like an elk head. He dug beneath the elk-shaped stone. As he dug, giant otters came out of the lake. At every thirteenth stroke of the miser's elkhorn pick, they struck the snow with their tails.

The miser continued digging. At sunset, he finally found a hollow holding all the hiaqua he could carry. He loaded himself with the strings of shells and began his descent. He did not even leave any as thanks on the elk-shaped rock.

As he left, the otters began to beat the water with their tails. A storm arose. Fleeing down the mountain, the miser heard behind him the beating of the tails and the wind laughing, "Ha, ha, hiaqua!" He became lost. The wind tugged at the load of shell money he carried. One by one, he began to throw the strings away. Each time he did, there was a slight lull in the storm. Finally, he threw away the last string and fell down exhausted in a faint.

When he awoke, the air was calm and the sun was shining. He was hungry, and his joints felt rusty and stiff. He touched his hair and found it long and matted.

He made his way down the volcano. In front of his lodge he saw an old woman, singing about her man who had gone up to the mountain and never returned. He sang a song in reply, and he and his wife recognized each other. He had been gone many years, she told him, and meanwhile she had grown rich trading bulbs and roots.

But her husband no longer cared for money. He became a wise man who told others of the best hunting places and the best ways to keep peace with the spirits.

The spirit-haunted mountains will end our world, so a Yakima tale says. Someday, the mountains will be overturned. The spirits of the dead, buried under the mountains, will go back to their bones. And the land will be flat again.

Nisqually Glacier flowing from the summit of Mount Rainier.

Indians and the Heights

Before the infringement of white settlers, the loosely knit Indian tribes of the Cascades — each tribe composed of several subgroups — wintered in permanent villages in foothill valleys or at the edges of the range. In summer, small groups of men followed game into the high country. Bears were caught in deadfall traps. Mountain goats were snared. (The Skagit tribe's spirit powers reputedly made them particularly skilled at this.) Whole villages moved into mountain valleys to traditional summer camping spots where men hunted, fished, traded, and gambled, and women gathered and dried roots, pine nuts, and berries. They carried with them summer dwellings either of skins or rush mats and poles. Lodgepole pine got its common name because its light, straight, and strong trunks were favored for these portable homes.

Alexander Ross, Canadian fur trader, described a giant camas-gathering camp on the upper Yakima River in 1814:

> Councils, root-gathering, hunting, horse-racing, foot-racing, gambling, singing, dancing, drumming, yelling, and a thousand other things which I cannot mention were going on. The din of men, the noise of women, the screaming of children, the tramping of horses and howling of dogs was more than can well be described.

Rapids, falls, and narrows where salmon were easily trapped or speared were favored for summer fishing camps. One was located at the mouth of Cle Elum Lake east of Snoqualmie Pass; another was near today's resort town of Packwood. The Klickitat Indians regularly crossed the low South Cascades in summer to trade and find food. You will find their name on Klickitat River and County east of the Cascades, and on Klickitat Creek and Prairie near Mossyrock west of the range.

An Indian fishes for salmon at Celilo Falls, now flooded by a reservoir.

The memory of wild harvesting spots is preserved in names like Camas Land, a plateau in the Wenatchee Mountains, and in Indian Heaven between Mount Adams and Mount Saint Helens, where the grooves worn by ponies' hooves can still be seen in the Indian racetrack. Indians and others still gather to harvest huckleberries in this area in late summer, but the crops are getting smaller. In the past, Indians regularly burned this and other areas to make hunting easier and to keep trees and brush from crowding out productive young plants. Today's strict control of forest fires accounts for the yield's decline, according to many foresters.

Indians traded a variety of goods across the mountains: wild hemp for fishnets, porcupine quills for decoration, mountain-goat wool, camas, dried salmon and clams, furs, horses, even slaves. Some tribes had close ties with their transmountain trading partners, sometimes marrying (or eloping) across the passes.

Indian racetrack, last used in the 1920s, is still etched in a meadow near Red Mountain. Mount Saint Helens is in the distance.

Indian trails seldom followed the routes of today's highways across the range. The Indians traveled as far as possible by dugout canoe, shooting mountain rapids with a steersman shouting directions to oarsmen who maneuvered the canoe with long poles. (They took up their paddles again in quiet water.) On land, their trails kept to high, narrow ridges where snow melted earlier and there were fewer streams and fallen logs to cross.

The main Indian trail through the Cascades wound through the Columbia's canyon. Otherwise, instead of crossing 3,004-foot Snoqualmie Pass, route of today's busiest highway through the range, Indians usually paddled up the Cedar River and crossed Yakima Pass, six miles south of Snoqualmie Pass and about 1,500 feet higher. Another major Indian water route extended up Lake Chelan for fifty-five miles, then crossed 5,900-foot White Pass to the Sauk River. Near today's town of Darrington, the narrow lowland between the Sauk and the Stillaguamish offered easy portage between the rivers.

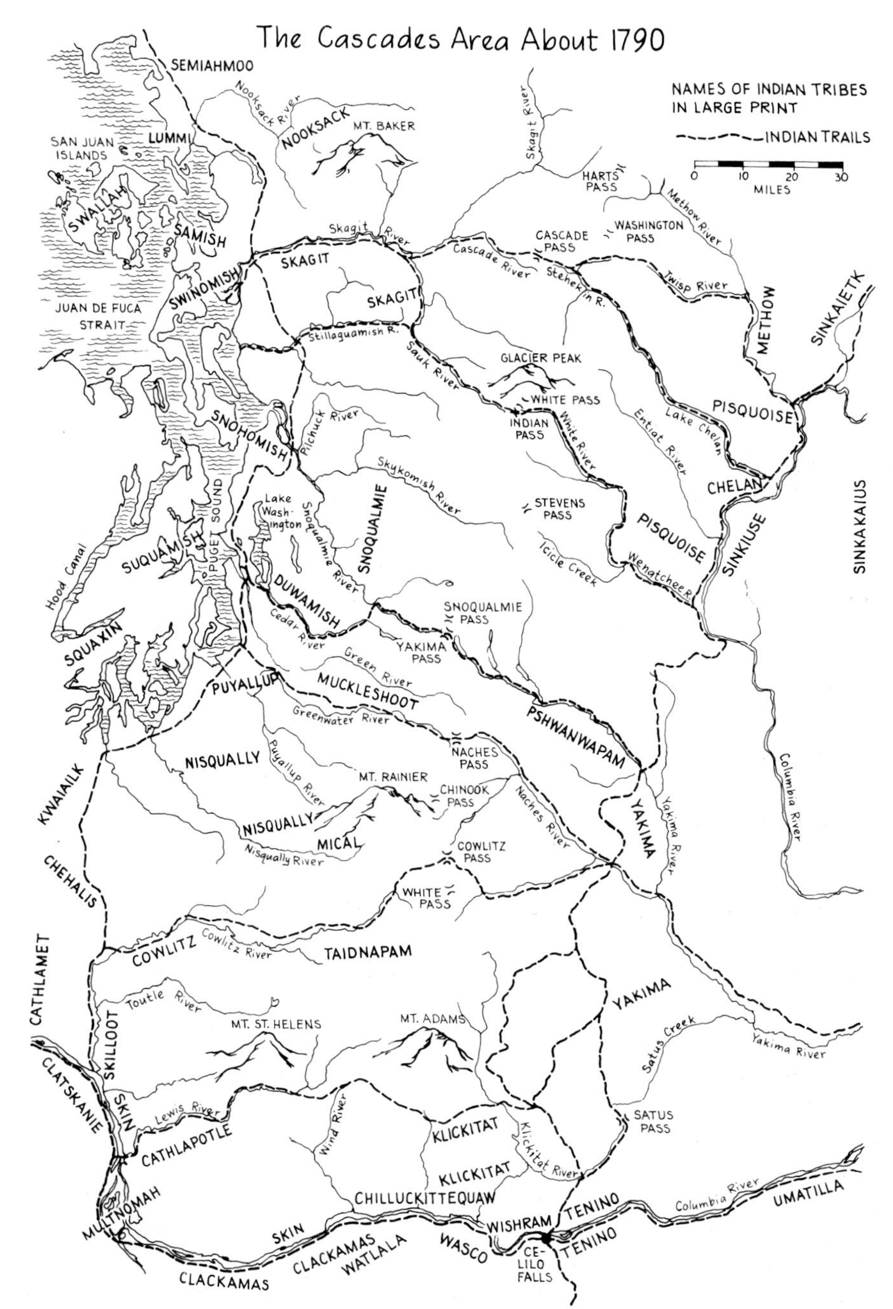

The Cascades before non-Indian settlement. (Compiled by the author from various sources. Modern geographic names have been provided for orientation.)

The Invaders

The first nonnatives to venture into Washington were explorers and motley bands of fur traders — Englishmen, French Canadians, Iroquois Indians, even Hawaiians. They became tough mountain men — and women. Alexander Ross, a fur trader then working for the British Northwest Company, was the first non-Indian to cross the Washington Cascades, in 1814. He probably followed the Indian trade route from eastern Washington across Cascade Pass, reaching the western foothills near the Skagit River before turning back because one of his Indian guides deserted him and another became ill.

Fur traders even drove cattle across the Washington Cascades. In 1841, both British Hudson's Bay Company employees and Yakima Indians drove cattle from inland trading posts across the South Cascades to company farms on the prairie south of Puget Sound. Such an agricultural enterprise was a sign that the fur trade era was over, killed by over-trapping and a fickle fashion change from beaver fur felt to silk hats. Another tide of American immigration that would profoundly change Washington and the Cascades was about to begin.

Though early explorers and fur traders were too few to fight the Indians, they decimated them nonetheless, with smallpox, venereal diseases, and other sicknesses for which the Indian had no natural immunity or herbal cures. By the 1850s, observers reported deserted villages along Cascade rivers and transmountain trails overgrown from lack of use.

By 1853, when Washington's first governor, Isaac I. Stevens, arrived in the new territory, Washington's non-Indian population was approaching 4,000. The area was ripe for clashes between Indian and immigrant.

Tribes living on the mountain fringes may have suffered most from Stevens's treaty making, aimed at concentrating Indians on reservations and opening the rest of the land to whites. Some bands, like those living on the upper Skagit, were not invited to Stevens's treaty conferences and were forced off their lands with no reservations. Others, like the Yakimas and the Wenatchees, were lumped together with their traditional enemies.

An Indian war broke out in 1855 because the Yakimas killed some prospectors crossing the Cascades on their way to a gold rush in Colville. They subsequently killed the agent who came to investigate and routed troops who came to subdue them. As hostilities increased, the mountains became more a refuge than a battleground. Even peaceful Indian bands sought safety in the foothills. There were massacres and brutalities on both sides. In 1856, Lieutenant (later General) A. V. Kautz recalled the rescue of some Nisqually Indians found hiding and near starvation in the western foothills. "Washington Territory volunteers had been before us, and with their immensely superior force had killed the most of them without regard to age or sex," he wrote.

In the eastern Cascades there were similar incidents. One army raid in the Wenatchee Mountains resulted in Indian families surrendering without a fight. However, one of the soldiers accidentally shot the troop commander. The troops then summarily hanged some braves, burned the Indians' lodges and belongings, and killed or stole their horses and cattle.

In 1858, the war dwindled. There were scattered "Indian scares" and even killings in the Cascade foothills through the next generation, as lone Indians or small groups tried to prove or protect themselves, or sought vengeance for thefts, lynchings, and rapes. Today the only visible remnants of Washington's one Indian war are scattered blockhouses and a peaceful square of buildings around a parade ground at Fort Simcoe, southwest of Yakima. Near the site of the war's first battle, strategically located at a favorite Indian camping spot on a major trade route, the fort symbolized that Washington and its Cascades were now white man's territory.

Wagons Cross the Mountains

Like the explorers and fur traders, Washington's first settlers generally avoided crossing the forbidding Cascades. They came either by sea, overland across Oregon's gentler Cascades, or through the Columbia's canyon.

With the first villages of rough wooden houses, the settlers seemed to want a road across the mountains. A road would draw more settlers, and more miners, they reasoned. Only a modest effort was needed: a trail wide enough for wagons, perhaps with split logs laid over the swampiest spots and a few crude bridges over streams. Ice Age glaciers had done much of the road work by cutting flat-bottomed valleys that formed low passes. Still, it was more than half a century before any road across the Cascades could be called a success.

Olympia was the first to try. In 1853, residents of the territorial capital donated a few thousand dollars and set out to build their own road following the old Indian route across nearby Naches Pass. They created a path of muck and a tangle of fallen trees, but did not reach the pass. Meanwhile, a wagon train that had started that spring from Indiana had heard the road would be built. By the time they found out otherwise, it was September and they were in the Cascades' eastern foothills. Fording the Naches River sixty-eight times, they forged ahead, lowering their wagons on rawhide ropes down the steep, 1,000-foot drop above Pyramid Creek on the west side. Finally, short of food, in torn clothes and worn-out boots, the James Longmire and James Biles party of more than 100 people became the first wagon train to cross the Washington Cascades.

The Naches Pass route was used again by a wagon train in 1854, by Indian and army troops during the Indian war, and by ranchers for cattle drives across the range. However, the many river crossings en route, to say nothing of the Pyramid Creek drop-off, made this a difficult wagon course. Although dreams of a highway with a four-mile tunnel through the range remained on the state's highway map into the 1970s, today the Naches Pass crossing is still a trail. It passes through woods and summit meadows much like those the pioneers found, and historic markers commemorate their wagon trains.

The historic Naches Pass wagon trail in terrain much like the pioneers found.

In 1859, a gold rush in eastern British Columbia spurred Snohomish County settlers to try to build their own road across Cady Pass, twelve miles north of today's Stevens Pass Highway. However, the mining rush dwindled, and Cady Pass remains a pleasant hike or horseback ride.

In the 1890s, the demands of goldminers and cattlemen convinced the new state of Washington to begin building a road across the jagged North Cascades. For the project, the legislature provided a bit less than $100 a mile. After starting out and giving up on an almost impossible route north of Mount Baker, and next rejecting the route of today's North Cascades Highway, builders turned again to an old Indian route. They actually did build a "road" up the Skagit and Cascade rivers, across Cascade Pass to the Stehekin Valley, up over Twisp Pass and down the Twisp River. This 1896 path served as a miner's trail but was never really good enough for wagons. Bridges were hard to build and maintain, so the road tended to end abruptly at rivers.

From Cascade Pass, a view of Mount Eldorado (left) and Forbidden Peak (right).

Although Seattle began promoting a road across Snoqualmie Pass in 1855, for years the route remained a rough trail crossed once a week by an Indian postman on horseback. Edmund T. Coleman, a British climber and artist who took the route in the early 1870s, told of a still-smoldering forest fire that frightened the party's horses near Issaquah. He also described mudholes east of the pass so deep that the horses had to scramble up the mountainside to get by. The pass itself, he described as "an open tract of turfy, marshy, meadow land . . . with here and there pools, bearing waterlilies, all hemmed in by the common red (Douglas) fir." In hollows there were cedars, their bark stripped off by Indians to make blankets.

After various attempts failed, Seattle businessmen tried a new tack to improve the road. In 1875 they lobbied a special bill through the legislature to let them hold a "grand lottery," selling 60,000 five-dollar tickets, with Henry Yesler's $100,000 sawmill as grand prize. However, ticket sales lagged, and the drawing was postponed until courts declared the lottery illegal. (The promoters seem to have fared better than the road: Yesler was fined twenty-five dollars, but the ticket money was not returned.)

The railroads that crossed the Cascades in the 1880s and 1890s quieted the citizens' clamor for roads. It was the automobile and the tourist that finally made the settlers' dream of a transmountain road come true. In 1909, the Snoqualmie Pass route was improved for a transcontinental auto race to promote Seattle's Alaska-Yukon-Pacific Exposition. The state maintained the road afterwards. The old highway, with roadside springs channeled into pipes to cool Model T radiators, can still be driven — it is known as the Denny Creek Road, just west of the pass.

Water trough found along the original Cascade Pass road.

Iron Roads

With railroads, as with roads, Washington's small settlements had do-it-yourself dreams. Everett businessmen planned tracks through Cady Pass. Goldendale and Pasco sought money for rails along the north bank of the Columbia. And Seattle businessmen twice set out to build their own rails across the Cascades. However, the time and place for railroads to cross the mountains was finally decided by larger forces. Although Washington Territory tried to compete for the first transcontinental railroad, California, with its alluring gold rush, became the hands-down winner. When a transcontinental train finally reached western Washington in 1883, it was ten years behind schedule because of the bankruptcy and reorganization of the Northern Pacific Railroad. In addition, its route was not what most Washington residents wanted: tracks followed the Oregon side of the Columbia Gorge, then turned north and ended at Tacoma, which was virtually a Northern Pacific company town.

Four years later, in 1887, the Northern Pacific laid the first tracks across the Washington Cascades and sent its first locomotive up the Yakima River, across Stampede Pass, and down the Green River — the route used by Amtrak trains today. It was a stormy undertaking. A drunken engineer let a flatcar jump the tracks and eight workmen were killed. Workers struck when wages were cut to two dollars a day. They "stampeded" down the mountain when a foreman announced a speed-up-or-don't-eat policy — thus giving Stampede Pass its name.

Compiled by the author from various sources.

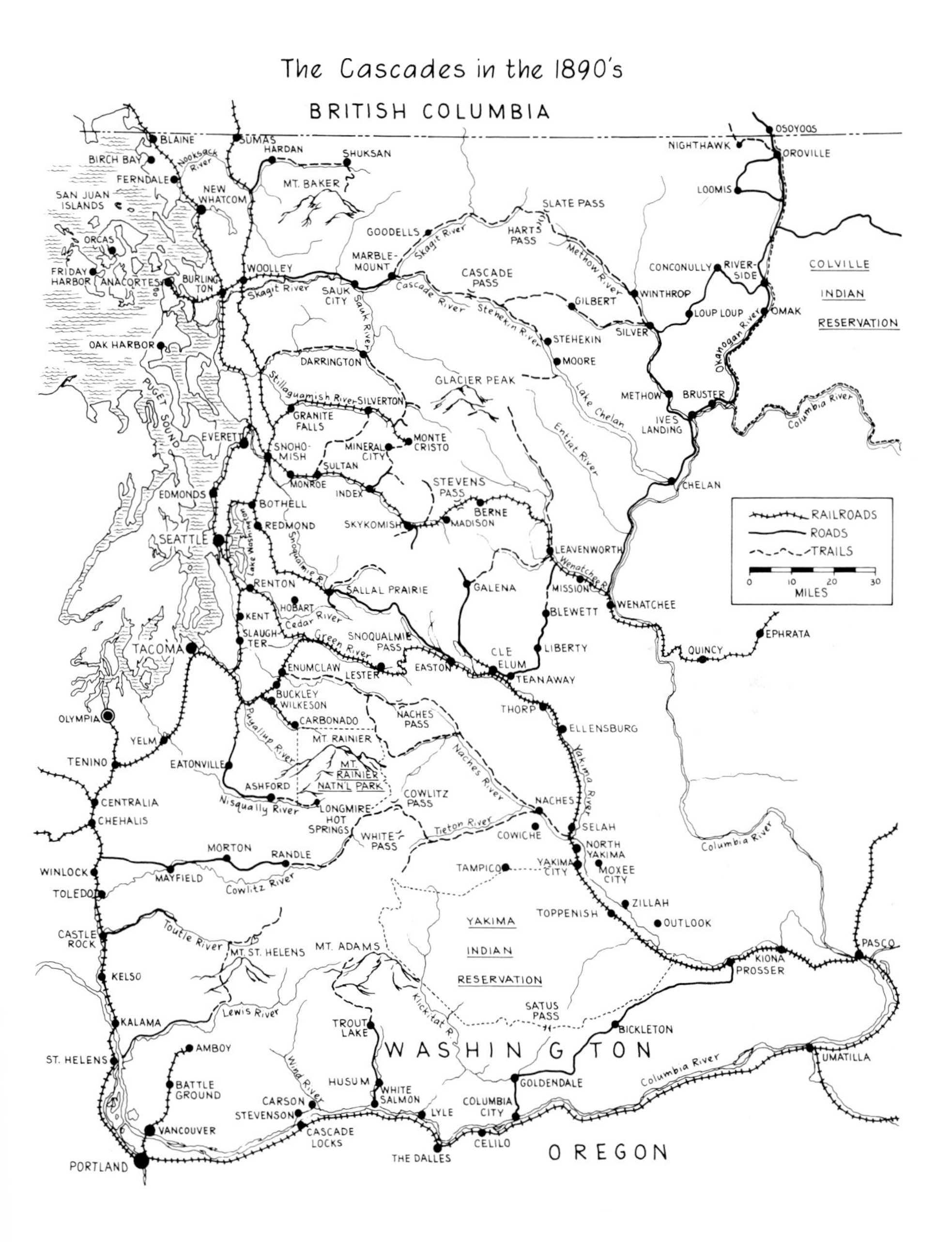

When the rails were new, homesteaders' cabins and clearings extended up the valley. Mining towns sprang up where the swamps of 50 million years before had turned into coal to fuel the locomotives. Coal towns on the west side of the range were Black Diamond, Carbonado, Ravensdale, Cumberland, and others. On the east were Cle Elum, Ronald, and picturesque Roslyn, with its old-fashioned storefronts, frame houses, and heaps of mine waste. Quiet now, they were once rough-and-tumble towns. Police in Black Diamond wore padded gloves with buckshot set in the knuckles. The town of Ronald burned when an illegal whiskey still in a basement blew sky-high.

Workers were Italian, Irish, Welsh, Yugoslav, Belgian, Chinese, and Afro-American. Sometimes one group was brought in to break another's strike, and feelings were by no means always friendly. In 1885, Chinese living quarters were burned during widespread anti-Chinese riots. When blacks were brought from the South to break strikes in Roslyn and Franklin, there were sympathy strikes throughout the mines. Many mines used child labor. Gravestones in the cemeteries tell of deadly explosions and fires, such as one at Roslyn that killed forty-five miners.

The second set of rails across the Washington Cascades — the Great Northern's tracks completed in 1893 across Stevens Pass — also changed the map of the Cascades. Stevens, White, and Carlton passes were named for intrepid railroad engineers who hiked these areas, searching for the best route. Rails brought big-time irrigation and fruit growing to Wenatchee and to Cashmere. The settlement of Icicle trundled buildings and all to the site where the Great Northern decided to build its shops, and thus Leavenworth was born. Boom towns of tents, shacks, and log cabins sprang up while the railroad was building: just east of the Stevens Pass tunnel was Tunnel City, christened in its brief heyday "the wickedest city in the world," with three bunkhouses, two whorehouses, two saloons, and almost no sanitation. More lasting were the lumber and mill towns that grew along the tracks on the west side of the range.

These were the days of trusts and trust-busting. Through an alliance with J.P. Morgan, James J. Hill, president of the Great Northern, acquired powerful influence over the Northern Pacific. The Northern Pacific in turn had a near monopoly through its purchases of smaller railroads and steamship lines in Washington. These two giants reached a compromise with the E.H. Harriman-Union Pacific interests in Oregon and California that would have made rails throughout the Pacific Northwest a virtual monopoly. In 1904, the United States Supreme Court ordered the breakup of this empire.

The flurry of competition that followed again changed the map of the Cascades. The Northern Pacific-Great Northern team financed tracks along the Washington shore of the Columbia Gorge, rivaling Union Pacific rails on the Oregon side. The Milwaukee Road completed its tracks across Snoqualmie Pass in 1909. The Union Pacific Railroad backed a plan to lay tracks up the Cowlitz River and down the Tieton, more or less along the route of today's White Pass Highway. Although the rails were never built, it is typical of the optimism of the day that some maps showed them as complete.

One postscript to the battle of the giants was the little town of Cliffs at the east end of the Columbia Gorge. Like many a boom town, Cliffs sprang up when the railroad planned facilities there and withered when the facilities went somewhere else. But Cliffs did not die. One of its abandoned hotels became a hobo jungle. Rustlers used the livery stable. An enterprising swindler did a fair business for a time ordering goods on stationery that the storekeeper had left behind. After lawmen cleared these citizens out, Cliffs became the county poor farm.

The completion of the Milwaukee Road tracks in 1909 — Washington's fourth and last set of tracks across the Cascades — marked the end of the twenty-five-year railroad boom in the state. The next year, 1910, the rails brought disaster.

The Great Northern's unventilated tunnel had threatened passengers with mass suffocation before trains passing through were electrified. Now a new disaster threatened. Sparks from locomotives burned broad belts along the tracks. Avalanches on the stripped mountainsides became more violent. In February, 1910, slides to the east and west halted a passenger train and a mail train for several days at Wellington station at the west portal of the Great Northern tunnel. About 2 A.M. March 2, an avalanche crashed down, tumbling both trains like toys into the ravine below. Ninety-six people were killed in Washington's worst rail disaster.

The Great Northern rebuilt the station with a new name, Tye, and with massive snowsheds protecting the tracks nearby. A new, 7.79-mile tunnel, still in use today, was completed in 1929. The old tunnel's west portal is a short walk down from the old Stevens Pass Highway, just north of the present highway. The huge concrete snowsheds still stand against the mountain. You can see cellar holes where buildings once stood. A few ties are still in place. Within a few feet of the tunnel entrance, streams trickling from the walls set up an eerie echo that sounds like an approaching ghost train.

Gold in Them Thar Hills

Like almost every western mountain range, the Cascades saw mining fevers in the late nineteenth and early twentieth centuries. However, the precious ores everyone thought so plentiful turned out to be scattered in small deposits, of low grade, or hard to refine. Few miners struck it rich.

There were ventures such as Peter Kirk's plan to mine iron just north of Snoqualmie Pass in the 1890s. Hoping to turn Seattle into the Pittsburgh of Puget Sound, he build the start of what would be the world's second largest ironworks at Kirkland, a Seattle suburb, before he discovered that the iron deposits were small and that local coal was not of the grade needed for smelting.

The 1930s witnessed an attempt to mine sulfur from the icy summit of Mount Adams, with mule trains and ski planes supplying men who climbed into crevasses and risked noxious sulfur fumes. Silver rushes occurred in the 1870s and 1880s, before silver was devalued in the panic of 1893. There were also some big copper mines: the Sunset Mine near Index; the Holden Mine on Railroad Creek, the Cascades' largest mine, which operated until the late 1950s. Its looming hills of rock waste are a reminder of conservationists' recurrent battles against mining a still larger deposit on Miners Ridge in the Glacier Peak Wilderness Area.

Most of the Cascade mining story is about the quest for gold. There is legend of a mysterious Spaniard who brought gold to the Columbia from somewhere near Mount Saint Helens in early territorial days. Skeletons believed to be those of the miner and his mules were found, but not his "lost mine."

Soldiers looking for a rail route across the Cascades in 1853 found traces of gold in the Yakima River drainage, the Cascades' first certain gold find. But "gold fever" did not sweep the territory until the 1858-1860 gold rush to eastern British Columbia and the Similkameem River in northeastern Washington. These mines soon dwindled, but the returning miners panned Cascade rivers from the Nooksack in the north to the Lewis in the south.

Some found gold in the Wenatchee Mountains, beginning a long and romantic mining era there. Driving the Blewett Pass Highway between Cle Elum and Wenatchee, you pass the remains of a stone grinder and the huge timbers of a stamp mill, both used to extract gold from stubborn ore. These are the only remains of the once-thriving mining settlement of Blewett. Creeks among these pine-covered slopes still yield nuggets to weekend panners. In nearby Liberty gold dredging continues; the gravel piles you see are tailings of the dredges.

Copper and gold mine at Holden above Lake Chelan.

The area has myths and memories of romance and violence. Ingalls Creek, south of Mount Stuart, has a "lost mine" legend. Supposedly a Captain Ingalls, lost in the mountains, found a rich gold vein in a deep valley cradling three lakes. But Ingalls was shot before he could return, and an earthquake buried the lakes. The Swauk Creek gold rush is supposed to have started when prospectors stopped to boil lice from their clothes and found gold in the wash water.

The miners were of many races and nationalities. Negro Creek was named for a black man who made a strike there. There were Chinese in pigtails and native dress: some were old sourdoughs who had come north from the California gold rush; others were fleeing the near slavery of work in salmon canneries. They had their own camps — one was at today's Salmon La Sac on the Cle Elum River. White miners persecuted them with everything from a special tax to ordering them out of the area, and there are tales that in 1875, Indians massacred Chinese miners on the banks of the Columbia near Chelan.

Miners ventured into the northeastern Cascades while the area was still Indian territory. In 1871, the U.S. Army drove inhabitants of a tent town called Chopaka City away from the foot of Mount Chopaka. After the Indian reservation was abolished in 1886, prospectors fanned out over the area and made strikes on the lower Methow River, on Salmon Creek near Conconully, near Palmer Mountain, and near today's Loup Loup ski area. Most of these boom areas never recovered from the panic of 1893, when silver was devalued, or from floods that swept away the raw mining towns in 1894.

Old mining debris at La Bohn Gap, ten miles from the nearest road.

As mining picked up again in the late 1890s, boom camps moved westward into the high Cascades. In 1895, Spokane's *Spokesman-Review* reported a rush to Squaw Creek, near the present town of Methow. "Every resident of Ruby except the postmaster has gone to Squaw Creek," the reporter declared. He went on to tell how an enterprising settler laid out a townsite of Ives Landing where the Methow River flows into the Columbia, and sold thirty-five lots to passengers arriving on the first steamboat from Wenatchee. (Ives Landing is today's Pateros.)

A rough wagon track built by miners is now the North Cascades Highway, its spur running northwest to Harts Pass. By 1903, this spur has seen five boom camps: Mazama, Ventura, Robinson, Barron, and Chancellor. There were mills, hotels, stores, and post offices to serve as many as 1,000 prospectors tenting in the hills. But the 3,000 or so claims produced only about $4 million in gold, most of it from only two mines. One of these, Alex Barron's Eureka Lode, is one of the few traces of the boom you can still see. Now called the New Lite Mine, its machinery and bulldozers are busy on the mountainside just off the Cascade Crest Trail.

The history of mining in the northeastern Cascades is similar. In the 1870s, there was a small silver rush to the narrow, ice-cut valleys northwest of Stevens Pass. Silver City, Galena, Mineral City, and other boom towns sprang up and died, leaving only their optimistic names on maps.

In the late 1870s, a group of hardy settlers ventured up the Indian trail along the Skagit and across the North Cascades because Indians had told them there might be gold in the peaks. They did find traces of gold. In the 1880 gold rush that followed, according to Otto Klement, a pioneer Skagit County merchant, 4,000 men risked winter avalanches on the narrow trail up the Skagit's canyon in order to arrive early. They laid out the town of Ruby on seventeen feet of snow, at the spot where Canyon and Granite creeks join to make Ruby Creek. (Today you pass the site on the North Cascades Highway.) Spring came late that year: mining began at last in August, and by the end of the month miners were down to bare rock with no sign of the "mother lode."

A miner's cabin at the abandoned Chancellor mining camp, at the junction of Slate and Canyon creeks.

State Highway 542 north of Mount Baker is a miner's trail followed by three prospectors who found the rich Lone Jack Mine near Twin Lakes. When news of the find got out, more than 1,000 miners clawed their way up the narrow trail, too steep in spots for pack animals. Five mining camps sprang up east of Glacier, today the easternmost settlement on the highway. At Shuksan, now a highway-maintenance depot, "Judge" John Broyles squatted on a claim and rented land he did not own to merchants and boomers, and also made a start on selling $2 million worth of stock in a mining company to city suckers. The town is said to have grown to two saloons, three stores, two boarding houses, and at least twenty dwellings in 1898. In spite of the booming, only two mines in the area made big money: the original Lone Jack find, and the nearby Boundary Red Mountain Mine, found accidentally by a mountain-goat hunter.

There were hopeful miners almost everywhere in the North Cascades during the 1890s and the first years of the twentieth century. Big companies packed in heavy machinery and built sawmills in the high, remote area between Cascade Pass and Lake Chelan. Picturesque Index, founded in 1890, boomed in 1891, burned and almost died in 1893, then boomed again in 1897. Silverton and Gold Basin over the next ridge north were frontier mining towns with hotels, saloons, and gamblers. Monte Cristo, a resort today, is believed to have produced about $7 million in gold without ever turning a profit for the J.D. Rockefeller-controlled syndicate that operated mills and mines.

South of these towns, between Stevens and Snoqualmie passes, most of the trails hikers enjoy today, including much of the Cascade Crest Trail, were built by prospectors and miners.

For all practical purposes, the Cascades gold fever died by about 1905. Perhaps the great gold rushes to Alaska and the Klondike between 1898 and 1904 drew men north and cured the fever with terrible cold and hardship. Perhaps the closing of the frontier ended a national dream of finding riches. Or miners may have realized that almost fifty years of combing the Cascades had produced relatively little.

Weekend prospectors and a few determined old men of the mountains still eke out a few dollars or look for the big strike. Occasionally, a hiker comes on remnants of the mining era — a tunnel, a ditch dug to wash gold, or heavy timbers and rusted machinery. For the most part, however, only hopeful names on maps — Quartz Creek, Silver Lake, Gold Basin — tell the casual visitor of the places where miners hoped to find their El Dorados.

Lone Jack Mine near Twin Lakes.

Timber-r-r!

The "gold" in the Cascades turned out to be green. The fir, spruce, hemlock, cedar, pine, and other cone-bearing trees that dominate Pacific Northwest forests have been Washington's largest industry since settlers began pouring into the territory in the 1850s.

At first, logging was a crude affair that could not venture far. Trees had to be chopped with axes. (The crosscut saw was an improvement of the 1870s.) Logs had to be floated to mills, or dragged by ox or horse teams over log "skid roads" greased with smelly dogfish oil.

By the 1880s, developments like log-pulling "donkey" steam engines, narrow-gauge logging railroads, and new transcontinental tracks across the Cascades made it possible to cut trees in what had been remote areas for shipment to distant markets. About the same time, the giant timber firms of the Midwest were realizing that their own hardwood forests would not last many more years. They began to look hungrily at the Pacific Northwest.

A rush for Cascade timber, akin to the gold rushes, followed. Timber stealing, waste, the giveaways of this period, and the crackdown that followed explain the pattern you see on maps of the Cascades today: easy-to-reach foothills and river valleys are owned privately, often by big timber companies. High mountains are public land — national forests or national parks. Yet over much of this public land runs a checkerboard of private ownership, stretching up to fifty miles on either side of the railroad tracks across Stampede Pass.

The checkerboard pattern was a congressional gift to the Northern Pacific Railroad to encourage it to build its transcontinental tracks. The land grant amounted to 25,000 acres for every mile of track the railroad built in Washington. (The Great Northern and the Milwaukee roads built without land grants.) Much of the Northern Pacific land was resold to private timber companies for a few dollars an acre. Frederick Weyerhaeuser, a shy German immigrant who had built a bankrupt Illinois lumberyard operation into a fortune in midwestern lumber, bought more than a million acres, moved his empire west, and became the state's largest private landowner.

The checkerboard pattern gives conservationists and land managers headaches today. For example, conservationists press the U.S. Forest Service to keep wild areas roadless, while private timber companies demand roads to log their squares in the checkerboard.

Much prime Cascade timberland passed into private hands through methods that were shady at best. Federal land laws designed to put small tracts in the hands of settlers were honeycombed with loopholes. The Land Office enforcing these laws was riddled with laxity and corruption. One

Working from springboards, lumberjacks cut down a Douglas fir in the Cascade foothills.

Felling a Douglas fir.

law, the Timber Culture Act, gave "settlers" a quarter of a square mile of land if they swore they had planted trees on part of it. The commissioner of the U.S. Land Office estimated in the 1880s that not 1 claim in 100 made under the act was made honestly.

Timber companies hired "settlers" to claim choice bits of forest under various laws. Pioneers who later became solid citizens wrote of first coming to the state to file a timber claim and make some quick money. Trainloads of schoolteachers were recruited to take a free vacation west, file timber claims, and resell the land to timber companies. In several Cascade valleys, the actual settlers were preceded by waves of timber claimants who staked out the best trees, sold wood or land to timber companies, then moved on.

The fast-disappearing forests of the East and Midwest and the timber barons' move westward sparked nationwide fears of monopoly and of a "timber famine." At the same time, the terrible waste of forest resources was strengthening the nation's first big conservation movement.

In Washington's Cascades as in much of the West, livestock of competing sheepmen and cowmen had grazed many meadows bare. Hunters for sport and market had decimated native herds of elk and mountain goats. Loggers followed destructive practices like that of corralling logs behind a "splash dam" that was then broken, sending wood and water downstream in a destructive mass that swept away riverside growth and ruined fish life.

And there was fire. A federal report in 1900 estimated that nearly eight percent of all the forests north of Mount Rainier had burned since the coming of the white man. Some fires were killers: a 1902 forest fire, thought to have been started by a prospector burning a log that blocked a trail, raged over 250,000 acres in the Cascades' southwestern foothills, killing thirty-five people.

Change came slowly. In 1891, Congress repealed the Timber Culture Act that had allowed some of the worst timber-land grabs. A Mount Rainier Forest Reserve was established in 1893. Then in 1897, in his last days in office, President Grover Cleveland abruptly stuck a "No Trespassing" sign on most of the public land left in the Cascades. There were howls of local protest, and President William McKinley modified boundaries and rules. But the reserves that became today's national forests remained, and law and order began to come to the forests. Still, rangers were not hired to administer the forest reserves until 1903, and a decade more passed before there was any effective control of forest fires.

The Farmer and the Cowman

The Yakima River and its tributaries fill valley after valley in the southeastern Cascades with lakes dammed for irrigation. The reservoirs are ugly and stump-rimmed in winter when they are low because farmers have used their water; but they are lovely blue playgrounds for motorboats in early summer, when they are filled with melted mountain snow not yet needed for crops.

These lakes represent the triumph of "sodbusters" who won the foothill valleys from stockmen, staked out more farms than the natural river could water, and then persuaded the federal government to bail them out.

Cattlemen brought livestock into the southeastern Cascades almost as soon as the Indian war ended. They moved gradually northward during the next thirty years until cattle grazed all along the eastern edge of the mountains. The land, still government owned, was open range at first where cattle roamed free except during the spring roundup, when each stockman branded the calves that followed his cows (and sometimes a few more). The cowboys were often Indians. Herds were driven to market in mining boom towns in Canada, Idaho, or Montana, or west over Snoqualmie and Naches passes to Puget Sound.

Cattle drive in the Okanogan area.

Cattlemen did not rule the range alone for long. Sheepmen soon followed; farmers arrived, who wanted the grazing land for their own cattle and used the new invention, barbed wire, to fence free-roaming herds out of their fields and gardens. With cattlemen, sheepmen, and farmers competing for the same highland meadows in summer, the same foothill grasslands in winter, grazing land grew bare and eroded from too many trampling hooves and nipping teeth. (Native tall bunchgrasses never recovered from this overgrazing. Shorter varieties seem to have replaced them permanently over most of the Cascade foothills.)

Into the early 1900s, range wars flared between cattlemen, sheepmen, and farmers on the east edge of the Cascades. There were whippings and hay burnings by hooded riders in the fight over whether cattle or sheep would graze the lush meadows near Mount Adams. Farmers along the Naches River fought herds of livestock being driven to pasture in 1898. They tried to turn the herds with stones, shouting, yelling, banging on cans, even a fiddle. Cowmen overturned farmers' fences. In retaliation, farmers butchered cows that wandered into their fields. The "battle" went on for a month. In the Okanogan area in 1903, tons of sheepmen's hay was burned. Armed raiders clubbed, shot, or axed almost a thousand sheep.

Financial panics and hard winters ruined many stockmen, but nothing could turn back the flood of farmers. They had legal title to the land. They had barbed wire. And they had numbers.

Sheep graze in Indian berry fields. Mount Saint Helens in background.

Settlers of the 1880s and 1890s on both sides of the Cascades lived the life pioneers faced everywhere in the nation. They cleared land with ax, hoe, and fire. They built log cabins and rough furniture: beds might be alder posts tied together, with moss mattresses. They swam their horses across swift Cascade rivers and ferried goods in dugout canoes. They put up with marauding animals, from pack rats to bears. They survived lean years, using wild berries for fruit and roasted wheat for coffee. They made wheat-straw hats, moccasins when they could not afford shoes, soap from fat and ashes, vinegar from wild honey. They salted and smoked meat and fish, raised their bread with sourdough. For recreation there were dances accompanied by fiddle and harmonica, and barn raisings and quilting bees that combined work and play.

Crops were varied: from hops along the Snoqualmie River to turkeys in the fertile Big Bottom of the Cowlitz near Randle. (Farmers drove the birds to Puget Sound markets, walking in daytime and letting them roost in trees at night.)

Along the southeastern Cascades, the fertile soil and long sunny days needed only water to make the desert bloom. The first irrigation systems were simply hand-dug ditches running a few hundred feet. The Yakima chief Kamaikin and Owhi watered their vegetable gardens this way from Ahtanum and Wenas creeks before the Indian war. In the foothills near Wenatchee, a black prospector called Big Antoine used the same ditch both to grow fruit and wash gold. This kind of irrigation spread in the 1870s and early 1880s.

With the coming of railways in the mid-1880s, firms backed by eastern capital moved in with ambitious schemes to irrigate thousands of acres, sell the land to settlers, and ship out huge crops by rail. Some succeeded. However, settlers lost their savings when canals were not built, or not maintained, or when water charges were suddenly boosted.

Fierce competition developed as the companies laid claim to more water than the rivers held. Union Gap Irrigation Company illegally built a dam on Cle Elum Lake. When a water shortage developed, Washington Irrigation Company dynamited it and destroyed another dam that diverted water onto the Yakima Indian Reservation.

A demand grew for the federal government to straighten out the mess. It did. In the early years of this century, the then-new Bureau of Reclamation bought the most important waterworks and set about turning natural glacial lakes and meadows into irrigation reservoirs. Bumping Lake was enlarged with a dam in 1910, Kachess Lake in 1912, Keechelus Lake in 1917. Meadows along the Tieton River where stockmen had grazed their cattle were flooded by dams to make Clear Lake in 1918 and Rimrock Lake in 1925. Cle Elum Lake was last, in 1933. The flourishing farms and orchards of the Yakima valley show that the "sodbusters" have triumphed.

Pioneer ranch of Joseph Morovitz below Mount Baker. It was built in 1890, some twenty-five miles from the nearest road.

The Scramble for Power

By the early years of the twentieth century, gold rushes and railroad booms had died away, and the scrambles for timberland and irrigation water were slowed by controls from the federal government. There was, however, one more "rush" to follow in the Cascades: the stampede for control of canyons and valleys where water could be trapped and put to work making electricity.

Governor Isaac I. Stevens probably echoed the typical settlers' sentiment in dismissing the rivers that flowed west from the Cascades with the comment: "They may be called ugly streams, all of them, and are a great obstruction to traveling in the country." But when the potential of cheap electric power came to the nation, these mountain rivers suddenly proved more valuable than all the gold ever found in the Cascades. Again, man exploited nature's work. Heavy rain and snow on the Cascades' western slopes provided a dependable water supply. At falls, at the rivers' narrow canyons, or in glacier-cut valleys that could be dammed, the mountain streams' power could be harnessed to turn turbines. In 1900, eight years after the first plants began generating and transmitting electricity in London and New York, Washington's first big hydroelectric project, the Snoqualmie Falls power plant, was completed. Its spectacular waterfall still produces power.

Before 1910, a new kind of prospector appeared in the Cascades — the water rights hunter. Under absurdly simple federal laws, he could stake out a claim to water rights on whole rivers and canyons, simply by tacking a notice to a tree and filing a claim at the local county courthouse. If he did not start work, someone else could file the same claim. Rival claims, and the long legal battles they started, sometimes decided where today's dams were or were not built.

There were promoters like fast-talking Rhodes "Water Rights" Green, who staked claims on the upper Cowlitz drainage, announced plans for a $7 million power project at Packwood Lake, and persuaded local settlers to move their Sulphur Springs post office to the new town of Lewis. The next spring workers arrived, but the company didn't.

In reality, only government or major utility companies had the money to harness the Cascade rivers. The fight for control of this power and wealth developed into a major political battle in the American West. Today, if you take Seattle City Light's boat tour of Ross Lake, or its shorter tours of Skagit dams and powerhouses, you will be seeing one of the big battlefields of this struggle.

Seattle started its electricity business in a small way in 1904, using the Cedar River, which supplied city drinking water, to light city streets. The development from this modest beginning to the big public utility that is now Seattle City Light is largely due to one man, James Delmage Ross.

Dunn Canyon of the Cowlitz River.

Ross ruled Seattle's electric utility from 1911 until his death in 1939. A gaggle of city councilmen and many a newspaper campaign tried to oust him. One mayor fired him: voters promptly recalled the mayor and Ross went back on the job. He was even allowed to keep his City Light position while serving the New Deal during the Great Depression of the 1930s.

Ross had almost unlimited faith in the benefits of electricity. He dreamed of electrifying the entire Great Northern Railway. He plunged into his job with characteristic energy — and disregard of the finer points of engineering. A high dam on the Cedar River was built despite engineering reports that warned water would leak out through loose Ice Age debris around the basin. Leak it did. The dam was next to useless.

Meanwhile, the private utility that was to become Ross's great rival was growing. Puget Sound Power and Light had bought the Snoqualmie Falls Project, built big dams and plants of its own, and seemed well on its way to becoming the major power source for western Washington. Great competition developed between the two for bond issues and bidding for sites. The City Light head became convinced that Puget Sound Power and Light was tying up dam sites to keep his public utility from expanding. He decided to go on the offensive. Secretly, he filed for rights to dam the Skagit, where Puget Sound Power and Light had held a permit to build for years.

The lower Skagit, largest of western Cascade rivers, is a broad stream flowing through fertile farmland. Above Marblemount its valley narrows suddenly, and the Skagit becomes a torrent rushing through a steep canyon. This torrent, if dammed, could produce vast amounts of electricity. After six years of claim conflicts, hearings, and delays, the first Seattle City Light dam on the Skagit, Gorge Dam, was finished in 1924. It cost the city more than twice original estimates. This dam in effect gave Seattle first claim on power sites higher up the river. Gorge Dam looks insignificant beside the engineering feats of later years: Diablo Dam, finished in 1930, and Ross Dam, finished in 1949.

Ross's legacy of a Seattle City Light dedicated to cheap and abundant power, and practically independent of the rest of city government, remains today. The utility has battled both conservationists and concerned Canadians in its plans to raise Ross Dam and flood the Skagit Valley farther into Canada.

Ross was buried, as he asked, beside his creation. His floodlit crypt has been one of the tourist attractions at the Skagit projects, along with a water wheel, a tram ride up a dam, a boat ride, and a walk along a trail with the mood enhanced in the evening by lights and recorded music. Ross probably would have approved — he wanted electricity to make people happy.

Colonial Peak and Diablo Lake, a Seattle City Light reservoir.

The Mountains Tomorrow

Stuart Range seen from the plexiglass cabin of a helicopter. Dragontail Peak, center.

Today's Washington Cascades are a partly tamed mountain range. Rivers are slowed by dams. Highways cross the passes. However, man's engineering feats have not prevented fatal avalanches or floods. Although man has made changes in the plant and animal communities — even in the shape of the mountains — his influence is minor when compared to the natural forces he cannot control: volcanic eruptions or climate changes that cause ice ages, for example.

Mountains that have endured ice caps and blankets of volcanic ash will probably survive man's influence. However, if only from our short-term point of view, it seems wise to be concerned about what we do to this backbone of Washington.

We face long-term unknowns. In a few hundred years, what will happen to Cascade plants and soils as a result of frequent clearcutting of timber and suppression of forest fire? There are big, pressing issues: Should large blocks of the range be logged and crisscrossed by roads, or remain almost unchanged as wilderness areas? Should new dams or highways be built?

We face a steady stream of small decisions with major cumulative effects. With each decision, values will be questioned: Will this alpine lakeshore be trampled bare by hooves and boots and strewn with campers' garbage? Will this trail be opened to noisy trail bikes?

In an area like the Cascades where we still scarcely understand complex community ties — such as how forests may depend on fungi — it seems wise at the very least to approach changes with caution. They could have unpredictable results.

Further Reading

Clark, Ella E. *Indian Legends of the Pacific Northwest.* Berkeley: University of California Press, 1953. A collection of many legends that makes good reading and sticks fairly close to the original Indian versions.

Easterbrook, Don J., and Rahm, David A. *Landforms of Washington.* Bellingham, Washington: Western Washington State College, Department of Geology, 1970. A nontechnical account of why Washington looks the way it does. Lots of photos.

Franklin, Jerry F., and Dyrness, C.T. *Vegetation of Oregon and Washington.* U.S.D.A. Forest Service Research Paper PNW-80. Portland, Oregon: U.S. Pacific Northwest Forest and Range Experiment Station, 1969. Language is technical, but this is probably the best explanation of local plant communities.

Haines, Aubrey L. *Mountain Fever: Historic Conquests of Rainier.* Portland: Oregon Historical Society, 1962. A book on early climbs with plenty of detail for those who climb and plenty of interesting quotations for those who don't.

Halliday, William R. *Caves of Washington.* Washington State Division of Mines and Geology Information Circular no. 40, 1963. Describes and maps most of the state's caves and warns of their dangers.

Harris, Stephen L. *Fire and Ice: The Cascade Volcanoes.* Seattle: Mountaineers and Pacific Search Books, 1976. Fascinating, easy-to-read geology.

Hitchcock, C. Leo, and Cronquist, Arthur. *Flora of the Pacific Northwest.* Seattle: University of Washington Press, 1973. A bit heavy to carry in a pack, but when you pass the beginning stage and learn to use a key, this comprehensive, well-illustrated manual is the best available guide for identifying local plants.

Ingles, Lloyd G. *Mammals of the Pacific States: California, Oregon, and Washington.* Stanford: Stanford University Press, 1965. An excellent guide that combines technical information and descriptions of range and habits.

Kozloff, Eugene N. *Plants and Animals of the Pacific Northwest.* Seattle: University of Washington Press, 1976. New, well-illustrated guide to the natural history of western Oregon, Washington, and British Columbia. Many color photos.

Larrison, Earl J. *Washington Mammals: Their Habits, Identification, and Distribution.* Seattle: Seattle Audubon Society, 1970. A good light, easy-to-carry local field guide with some information about habits.

Larrison, Earl J., and Sonnenberg, Klaus. *Washington Birds: Their Location and Identification.* Seattle: Seattle Audubon Society, 1968. A good local field guide best used with a better-illustrated book if you are a beginner.

Livingston, Vaughn E. *Fossils in Washington.* Washington State Division of Mines and Geology Information Circular no. 33, 1959. A beginning guide for the fossil hunter.

Lyons, Chester P. *Trees, Shrubs and Flowers to Know in Washington.* Toronto: J.M. Dent and Sons, 1956. In my opinion, the best beginning field guide to local plants available.

McKee, Bates. *Cascadea: The Geologic Evolution of the Pacific Northwest.* New York: McGraw Hill Book Company, 1972. If you can get through the technical language, this is a fascinating and informative account of what is known and is not known about the region's geology.

McKenny, Margaret. *The Savory Wild Mushroom.* (Revised and enlarged by Daniel E. Stuntz). Seattle: University of Washington Press, 1971. Probably the best local beginning guide of the many mushroom guides available.

Meany, Edmond S. *History of the State of Washington.* New York: Macmillan, 1942. Basic history.

Mohney, Russ. *Why Wild Edibles? The Joys of Finding, Fixing, and Tasting – West of the Rockies.* Seattle: Pacific Search Books, 1975. A good introduction to edible wild plants and their preparation for the palate.

Mountaineers. *Mountaineering: The Freedom of the Hills.* Seattle: Mountaineers, 1974. Hard-to-beat guide on safety and basic techniques of hiking and climbing.

Murie, Olaus. *A Field Guide to Animals Tracks.* 2d edition. Boston: Houghton Mifflin Company, 1954. Excellent field guide to tracks and other animal signs.

Peterson, Roger T. *A Field Guide to Western Birds.* 2d edition. Boston: Houton Mifflin Company, 1969. Very good field guide, with birdsong records to match if you want them.

Pyle, Robert M. *Watching Washington Butterflies.* Seattle: Seattle Audubon Society, 1974. Charming handbook on a delightful subject.

Schroeder, Mark J., and Buck, Charles C. *Fire Weather: A Guide for Application of the Meteorological Information to Forest Fire Control Operations.* U.S. Forest Service Agriculture Handbook no. 360, 1970. An excellent summary of mountain weather, in simple language, with clear charts and diagrams.

Spring, Bob and Ira, and Manning, Harvey. *102 Hikes in the Alpine Lakes, South Cascades, and Olympics.* Seattle: Mountaineers, 1971 — and other books in the Mountaineers' "hike" series. These tour guides for backpackers describe trails, scenery, camping spots; estimate difficulty and hiking time; recommend the best visiting seasons; tell elevation gains and altitudes; and illustrate it all with photos and sketch maps.

Tarling, Donald H. and M.P. *Continental Drift: A Study of the Earth's Moving Surface.* London: G. Bell and Sons, 1971. One of several easy-to-read books on continental drift.

Taylor, Thomas M.C. *Pacific Northwest Ferns and Their Allies.* Toronto: University of Toronto Press, 1970. A little large for a backpack but an excellent book for identifying ferns, horsetails, and club mosses.

Yocom, Charles F., and Brown, Vinson. *Wildlife and Plants of the Cascades: Covering Most of the Common Wildlife and Plants of the Pacific Northwest and the Area of Lava Beds.* Healdsburg, California: Naturegraph Publishing, 1971. Does a good job of combining plants and animals in a single handbook. Necessarily incomplete but easy to use. A good field guide for beginners who have no specialized interests.

Zwinger, Ann H., and Willard, Beatrice E. *Land Above the Trees: American Alpine Tundra.* New York: Harper, 1972. Beautifully written and illustrated.

Other Pacific Search Books in Paperback

Bone Appétit! Natural Foods for Pets by Frances Goulart. Meatless morsels for cats, dogs, and cooks! Drawings. 96 pp. $2.95.
Butterflies Afield in the Pacific Northwest by William Neill/Douglas Hepburn, photography. Lovely guide with 74 unusual color photos of living butterflies. 96 pp. $5.95.
The Carrot Cookbook by Ann Saling. Over 200 mouth-watering recipes. 160 pp. $3.50.
The Dogfish Cookbook by Russ Mohney. Over 65 piscine delights. Cartoons and drawings. 108 pp. $1.95.
Fire and Ice: The Cascade Volcanoes by Stephen L. Harris. Copublished with The Mountaineers. Black-and-white photos and drawings, maps. 320 pp. $7.50.
The Green Tomato Cookbook by Paula Simmons. More than 80 solutions to the bumper crop. 96 pp. $2.95.
Living Shores of the Pacific Northwest by Lynwood Smith/Bernard Nist, photography. Fascinating guide to seashore life. Over 140 photos, 110 in color. 160 pp. $9.95.
Minnie Rose Lovgreen's Recipe for Raising Chickens by Minnie Rose Lovgreen. 2d edition. 32 pp. $2.00.
Sleek & Savage: North America's Weasel Family by Delphine Haley. Extraordinary color and black-and-white photos; bibliography. 128 pp. $5.50.
Toothed Whales: In Eastern North Pacific and Arctic Waters compiled by Alice Seed. 2d edition. 40 pp. $1.75.
Why Wild Edibles? The Joys of Finding, Fixing, and Tasting – West of the Rockies by Russ Mohney. Color and black-and-white photos plus illustrations. 320 pp. $6.95.
Wild Mushroom Recipes by the Puget Sound Mycological Society. 2d edition. Over 200 recipes. 178 pp. $6.95.
The Zucchini Cookbook by Paula Simmons. Revised and enlarged 2d edition. Over 150 tasty creations. 160 pp. $3.50.